The Dome of Provisions

Part 1

The Dome of Provisions
Part 1

Spiritual Discourses of
Shaykh Muhammad Hisham Kabbani

PUBLISHED BY THE
INSTITUTE FOR SPIRITUAL AND CULTURAL ADVANCEMENT

© Copyright 2012 by Institute for Spiritual and Cultural Advancement.

Printed and bound in the United States of America. All rights reserved. No part of this book may be reproduced in any form or by any electronic or mechanical means, including information storage and retrieval systems, without permission in writing from the publisher, except by a reviewer, who may quote brief passages in a review.

Published and Distributed by:

Institute for Spiritual and Cultural Advancement (ISCA)
17195 Silver Parkway, #201
Fenton, MI 48430 USA
Tel: (888) 278-6624
Fax: (810) 815-0518
Email: staff@naqshbandi.org
Web: http://www.naqshbandi.org

First Edition: MAY 2012
THE DOME OF PROVISIONS, PART 1
ISBN: 978-1-930409-87-3

Library of Congress Cataloging-in-Publication Data

Kabbani, Muhammad Hisham.
Spiritual discourses of Shaykh Muhammad Hisham Kabbani. -- 1st ed.
p. cm. – "The Dome of Provisions, Part 1"
Includes bibliographical references.
ISBN 978-1-930409-87-3 (alk. paper)
1. Naqshabandiyah. 2. Sufism. I. Title.
BP189.7.N352K327 2012
297.4'8--dc22
   2010044186

PRINTED IN THE UNITED STATES OF AMERICA
15 14 13 12 11 05 06 07 08 09

Mawlana Shaykh Hisham Kabbani leads *dhikr*, "God remembrance" or meditation, in the renowned Naqshbandi *zawiya* in Michigan. (2010)

Table of Contents

About the Author i
Preface iii
Publisher's Notes v
Masters of the Naqshbandi-Haqqani Golden Chain ix
Recitation Before Every Association xi
What Holy Qur'an Says About the Saints xiii
What Is the Dome of Provisions? 1
   Your Password Opens Your Trust 2
   Secrets of the Dome of Provisions 5
From Whom Can We Take Tariqah? 7
   The Shaykh's Protective Shield 8
   Hit the Rock of the Ego to Get Your Spiritual Provision 10
   Shaykh Ahmad al-Badawi and the Key 13
   When You Submit to Your Shaykh 15
   The Shaykh From Whom You May Take 21
The Threat of an Eloquent Hypocrite 25
   The Nature of Hypocrites 25
   The Real Wali Gives to You from the Heart of the Prophet 28
   Your Spiritual Blueprint 30
   Why the Live Broadcast Is Delayed 32
Benefits of the Halaqah (Dhikr Circle) 35
   Your Qiblah Is Your Shaykh 36
   Conditions of a Heavenly Circle 40
   Three Halaqahs of Shah Naqshband 41
The Power of Intercession 45
   Miracles of Awliyaullah 45
   The Power of Dhikrullah 47
There Is No Rest in Religion 53
   How to Enter Maqam al-Ihsan 54
Stories of Awliya and Their Murids: `Ubaydullah al-Amawi 57
   The Evolution of Naqshbandi Tariqah 58
   The Central Role of Obedience in Spiritual Development 60
   The Wrestler Who Submitted 62
   When the Shaykh Opens Your Trust 65
   Embracing the Six Articles of Faith 70
   The Coveted Ocean of Moral Excellence 72
   There Are No Questions in Tariqah! 75
   About Those Who Accepted the Trust 80
   The Atom of Sayyidina Muhammad's Creation 82
   What Answered Allah on the Day of Promises? 84

The Three Realities of Every Human Being..................................86
The Wrestler Who Took His Trust 89
How to Destroy Black Magic..93
`Abdul-Khaliq's Question that Ended the Debate..........................94
The First Steps of Submission..97
The Demolition Room..101
The Sajda Under the Throne of Allah 105
Five Magnificent Favors Allah Grants in Ramadan 109
Prophet Foretold 360 Energy Points 113
Supplications that Replace Badness with Goodness....................114
The Adab of Eating 117
Take Each Bite with "Bismillah"..................................118
The Harm of Hungry Eyes 119
Bread Is from Heavens, So Honor It! 121
The Sin of Breaking the Fast of Ramadan Too Soon 123
Islamic Calendar and Holy Days 125
Glossary 129
Other Publications 135

About the Author

Shaykh Kabbani is a renowned religious scholar of both traditional Islamic law and the spiritual science of Sufism. He hails from a respected family of traditional Islamic scholars, which includes the former head of the Association of Muslim Scholars of Lebanon and the present Grand Mufti (highest Islamic religious authority) of Lebanon. In addition, he trained under the revered Shaykh 'AbdAllah al-Fa'iz ad-Daghestani of Damascus (d. 1973), and his successor, Shaykh Muhammad Nazim Adil al-Haqqani of Cyprus.

For three decades, he has promoted traditional Islamic principles of peace, love, compassion and social cohesion, while rigorously opposing extremism. As deputy leader of the Naqshbandi-Haqqani Sufi Order, he is authorized to issue religious edicts and counsel students of the movement, which is worldwide.

Since the early 1990s, Shaykh Kabbani has been pivotal in helping non-Muslim societies understand the difference between moderate mainstream Muslims and minority extremist sects.

In 2010, the Shaykh hosted HRH Prince Charles of Wales. He has hosted two international conferences in the U.S. and various regional conferences around the world. His counsel is sought by journalists, academics, policymakers, community leaders and activists.

In the United States, Shaykh Kabbani serves as Chairman, Islamic Supreme Council of America; Founder, Naqshbandi Sufi Order of America; Advisor, World Organization for Resource Development and Education; and Chairman, As-Sunnah Foundation of America. In the United Kingdom, Shaykh Kabbani founded the Centre for Spiritual and Cultural Advancement and is lead scholar for the Sufi Muslim Council, a non-profit NGO that consults to the British government on public policy and social and religious issues. He has launched popular websites, such as eShaykh.com, SufiLive.com, spiritandculture.org.uk and islamicsupremecouncil.org.

Shaykh Kabbani has written numerous books on Islamic spirituality. He is well known in policy development circles and has presented several critical position papers on the current state of global Islam, counter-terrorism, and the primacy of democratic principles in Islam. In 2011, the Shaykh issued an unprecedented *fatwa*, *The Prohibition of Domestic Violence in*

Islam, (ISBN 9781930409972) which cites Islamic texts that condemn family violence.

Other titles by Shaykh Kabbani include: *The Sufilive Series* (2010-2012, 6 vols.), *At the Feet of My Master* (2010, 2 vols.), *The Nine-fold Ascent* (2009), *Banquet for the Soul* (2008), *Illuminations* (2007), *Universe Rising* (2007), *Symphony of Remembrance* (2007), *A Spiritual Commentary on the Chapter of Sincerity* (2006), *The Sufi Science of Self-Realization* (Fons Vitae, 2005), *Keys to the Divine Kingdom* (2005), *Classical Islam and the Naqshbandi Sufi Order* (2004), *The Naqshbandi Sufi Tradition Guidebook* (2004), *The Approach of Armageddon? An Islamic Perspective* (2003), *Encyclopedia of Muhammad's Women Companions and the Traditions They Related* (1998, with Dr. Laleh Bakhtiar), *Encyclopedia of Islamic Doctrine* (7 vols. 1998), *Angels Unveiled* (1996), *The Naqshbandi Sufi Way* (1995), *and Remembrance of God Liturgy of the Sufi Naqshbandi Masters* (1994).

Preface

This book is based on the *suhbah*, extemporaneous, divinely inspired discourses of Shaykh Muhammad Hisham Kabbani, disciple and representative of the global head of the Naqshbandi-Haqqani Sufi Order, Mawlana Shaykh Nazim Adil al-Haqqani.

The Dome of Provisions, known in Arabic as "*Qubbat al-Arzāq*," refers to a sacred place under God's Throne that is only accessible by His chosen ones. It is the main source of heavenly secrets sent to the hearts of people, and is a divine store of blessings.

This two-volume collection of spiritual discourses is based on ancient teachings of Sufi masters of the renowned Naqshbandi Golden Chain, which dates back to Prophet Muhammad, may the peace of God be upon him. These particular discourses, presented in two volumes, were featured in the author's highly coveted discourses "Ramadan Series 2009." Lessons outline the mind-body-spirit connection and inspire readers to "Maqam al-Ihsan," the Station of Moral Excellence, in which one surrenders the ego and personal desires to Divine Will. Memorable accounts of previous masters and their disciples, the struggles they faced and the lofty heights they reached rounds out this work.

Basic knowledge of Sufi principles is recommended; however, one need not be a current traveler on the Sufi Path to benefit from the lessons in this book.

For fifty years, the author has sought to serve his master and promote these ancient Sufi teachings in the best manner. We hope *The Dome of Provisions* reflects this spirit and lays to rest any confusion about the Greatness of Prophet Muhammad, unto him be peace, and the roles, responsibilities, accomplishments and miracles of past saints and those who live among us even now.

It is said whomever mentions the name of one of God's saints is immediately blessed by that holy soul, and we pray this book generates such blessings.

❧ iv ☙

Publisher's Notes

This book is directed to those familiar with the Sufi Way; however, to accommodate lay readers unfamiliar with Sufi terminology and practices, we have provided English translations of Arabic texts and a comprehensive glossary. Where Arabic terms are crucial to the discussion, we have included transliteration and explanations. For readers familiar with Arabic and Islamic teachings, for further clarity please consult the cited sources.

The original material is based on transcripts of a series of holy gatherings known as *suhbah*, a divinely inspired talk given by the "Shaykh," a highly trained spiritual guide. To present the authentic flavor of such rare teachings, great care was taken to preserve the speaking styles of both the author and the illustrious Shaykhs upon whose notes this book is based.

Translations from Arabic to English pose unique challenges that we have tried our best to make understandable to Western readers. Please note our application of the common Arabic oral tradition of omitting definite articles such as "~~the~~ Prophet" and "~~the~~ Holy Qur'an," as practiced by Muslims around the world as intimate references.

Quotes from the Holy Qur'an and Holy Traditions of Prophet Muhammad are offset, italicized and cited.

The pronoun "they" is frequently used by Sufi guides to reference heavenly beings and holy souls who support them and give them orders, a usage that appears throughout this book. Where gender-specific pronouns such as "he" and "him" are applied in a general sense, no discrimination is intended towards women, upon whom The Almighty bestowed great honor.

Islamic teachings are primarily based on four sources, in this order:

- **Holy Qur'an**: The Islamic holy book of divine revelation (God's Word) granted to Prophet Muhammad. Reference to Holy Qur'an appears as "4:12," which indicates "Chapter 4, Verse 12."

- **Sunnah**: Holy traditions of Prophet Muhammad ﷺ; the systematic recording of his words and actions that comprise the *hadīth*. For fifteen centuries, Islam has applied a strict, highly technical standard, rating each narration in terms of its authenticity and categorizing its "transmission." As this book is not highly technical, we simplified the reporting of *hadīth,* but included the narrator and source texts to support the discussion at hand.

ࡳ **Ijma':** The adherence, or agreement of the experts of independent reasoning *(āhl al-ijtihād)* to the conclusions of a given ruling pertaining to what is permitted and what is forbidden after the passing of Prophet Muhammad, peace be upon him, as well as the agreement of the Community of Muslims concerning what is obligatorily known of the religion with its decisive proofs. Perhaps a clearer statement of this principle is, "We do not separate (in belief and practice) from the largest group of the Muslims."

ࡳ **Legal Rulings:** Highly trained Islamic scholars form legal rulings from their interpretation of the Qur'an and the Sunnah, known as *ijtihād.* Such rulings are intended to provide Muslims an Islamic context regarding contemporary social norms. In theological terms, scholars who form legal opinions have completed many years of rigorous training and possess degrees similar to a doctorate in divinity in Islamic knowledge, or in legal terms, hold the status of a high court or supreme court judge or higher.

The following universally recognized symbols have been respectfully included in this work. While they may seem tedious, they are deeply appreciated by the vast majority of our readers.

ﷻ *subhanahu wa Ta'alā* (may His Glory be Exalted), recited after the name "Allah" and any of the Islamic names of God.

ﷺ *sallAllahu 'alayhi wa sallam* (God's blessings and greetings of peace be upon him), recited after the holy name of Prophet Muhammad.

؏ *'alayhi 's-salam* (peace be upon him/her), recited after holy names of other Prophets, names of Prophet Muhammad's relatives, the pure and virtuous women in Islam and angels.

؇/؆ *radiAllahu 'anh(um)* (may God be pleased with him/her), recited after the holy names of Companions of Prophet Muhammad; plural: *radiAllahu 'anhum.*

ق represents *qaddasAllahu sirrah* (may God sanctify his secret), recited after names of saints.

Transliteration

Transliteration from Arabic to English poses challenges. To show respect, Muslims often capitalize nouns that in English appear in lowercase.

To facilitate authentic pronunciation of names, places and terms, use the following key:

Symbol	Transliteration	Symbol	Transliteration	Vowels: Long	
ء	ʾ	ط	ṭ	آ ى	ā
ب	b	ظ	ẓ	و	ū
ت	t	ع	ʿ	ي	ī
ث	th	غ	gh	Short	
ج	j	ف	f	ˊ	a
ح	ḥ	ق	q	ʼ	u
خ	kh	ك	k	ˎ	i
د	d	ل	l		
ذ	dh	م	m		
ر	r	ن	n		
ز	z	ه	h		
س	s	و	w		
ش	sh	ي	y		
ص	ṣ	ة	ah; at		
ض	ḍ	ال	al-/'l-		

Masters of the Naqshbandi-Haqqani Golden Chain

May Allah ﷻ preserve their secrets.

1. Prophet Muhammad ibn 'AbdAllah ﷺ
2. Abu Bakr as-Siddīq ق
3. Salman al-Farsi ق
4. Qasim bin Muhammad bin Abu Bakr ق
5. Jafar as-Sādiq ق
6. Tayfur Abu Yazīd al-Bistāmi ق
7. AbulHassan 'Ali al-Kharqani ق
8. Abu 'Ali al-Farmadi ق
9. Abu Yaqūb Yusuf al-Hamadani ق
10. AbulAbbas, al-Khidr ق
11. 'Abdul Khaliq al-Ghujdawāni ق
12. Arif ar-Riwakri ق
13. Khwaja Mahmūd al-Anjir al-Faghnawi ق
14. 'Ali ar-Ramitani ق
15. Muhammad Baba as-Samasi ق
16. as-Sayyid Amir Kulal ق
17. Muhammad Bahauddin Shah Naqshband ق
18. Ala'uddin al-Bukhari al-Attar ق
19. Yaqūb al-Charkhi ق
20. Ubaydullah al-Ahrar ق
21. Muhammad az-Zahid ق
22. Darwish Muhammad ق
23. Muhammad Khwaja al-Amkanaki ق
24. Muhammad al-Baqi billah ق
25. Ahmad al-Farūqi as-Sirhindi ق
26. Muhammad al-Masum ق
27. Muhammad Sayfuddin al-Farūqi al-Mujaddidi ق
28. as-Sayyid Nur Muhammad al-Badawani ق
29. Shamsuddin Habib Allah ق
30. 'AbdAllah ad-Dahlawi ق
31. Khalid al-Baghdadi ق
32. Ismail Muhammad ash-Shirwāni ق
33. Khas Muhammad Shirwāni ق
34. Muhammad Effendi al-Yaraghi ق
35. Jamaluddin al-Ghumuqi al-Husayni ق
36. Abu Ahmad as-Sughuri ق
37. Abu Muhammad al-Madani ق
38. Sharafuddin ad-Daghestani ق
39. 'AbdAllah al-Fa'iz ad-Daghestani ق
40. Muhammad Nazim Adil al-Haqqani ق

※ × ※

Recitation Before Every Association

*A'ūdhu billāhi min ash-Shaytan ir-rajīm.
Bismillāhi' r-Raḥmāni 'r-Raḥīm.
Nawaytu 'l-arbā'īn, nawaytu 'l-'itikāf,
nawaytu'l-khalwah, nawaytu 'l-'uzlah,
nawaytu 'r-riyaḍa, nawaytu 's-sulūk,
lillāhi Ta'alā fī hādhā 'l-masjid.*

*Ati'ūllāha wa ati' ūr-Rasūla
wa ūli'l-amri minkum.*

*I seek refuge in Allah from Satan, the rejected.
In the Name of Allah, the Merciful,
the Compassionate.
I intend the forty (days of seclusion);
I intend seclusion in the mosque,
I intend seclusion, I intend isolation,
I intend discipline (of the ego); I intend to travel
in God's Path for the sake of God,
in this mosque.*

*Obey Allah, obey the Prophet,
and obey those in authority among you.
Suratu 'n-Nisā (The Women), 4:59*

xii

What Holy Qur'an Says About the Saints

أَلا إِنَّ أَوْلِيَاءَ اللَّهِ لَا خَوْفٌ عَلَيْهِمْ
وَلَا هُمْ يَحْزَنُونَ

'Alā inna awliyaullahi
lā khawfun 'alayhim wa lā hum yahzanūn.

*Behold! Verily on the Friends of Allah (saints)
there is no fear, nor shall they grieve.*

Holy Qur'an: Jonah, 10:62

What Is the Dome of Provisions?

*A'ūdhu billāhi min ash-Shaytani 'r-rajīm. Bismillāhi' r-Raḥmāni 'r-Raḥīm.
Nawaytu 'l-arbā'īn, nawaytu 'l-'itikāf, nawaytu'l-khalwah, nawaytu 'l-'uzlah,
nawaytu 'r-riyaḍa, nawaytu 's-sulūk, lillāhi Ta'alā fī hādhā 'l-masjid.
Ati'ūllāha wa ati'ū 'r-Rasūla wa ūli 'l-amri minkum.
Obey Allah, obey the Prophet, and obey those in authority among you. (4:59)*

The Dome of Provisions, known in Arabic as "*Qubbat al-Arzāq,*" is hidden under `Arshullah, Allah's Heavenly Throne. Allah ﷻ gave it to Prophet Muhammad ﷺ, along with all the angels Allah created up to the Day of Judgment. They remain under the command of Prophet ﷺ so they can reach everyone, to present the provisions to human beings and to living and non-living beings.

SubhanAllah. Every drop of water that falls on a river or ocean is moved by angels from under that heavenly dome. That is why Prophet said, '*Ana al-Qassim wa 'ana al-Mahiy wa 'ana TaHa wa YaSin,*" "I am Qassim and I am al-Mahiyy and I am Taha and YaSin[1] —the one who divides provision to you, both physical and spiritual. Allah gave me that authority. I am the one who makes sure your provisions reach you from that dome and I am the one who erases."

Don't you think Prophet ﷺ is erasing our sins? If you don't think that, then your *iman* is not yet strong.

For our *rizq*, physical provision, Allah ﷻ assigned every bite you eat to angels that take it all the way through your system. Both groups of angels are under the command of Sayyidina Muhammad ﷺ: those who are in charge of each bite of your food, and those who bring inspirations to your heart and fill you with spiritual knowledge.

The angels that fill you with spiritual knowledges download them to your heart, but veil them from your mind. Your heart can take them in, but your mind cannot read them because they are 'password protected'. That password comes with your five pillars of Islam, the six pillars of *Iman* and the one pillar of *Ihsan*.

---

[1] An authentic hadith

Sayyidina `Umar ؓ mentioned the hadith that a man appeared in front of the *masjid*, entering the presence of Prophet ﷺ. He was someone they didn't know, a stranger. In the end, Prophet ﷺ said, "It was Jibrīl ؑ; he came to teach you your religion." So this means that religion is within this hadith. Jibrīl ؑ asked Prophet ﷺ about three issues on religion that complete each other: *man islam wa man imān wa man ihsān*. You cannot take one and leave the rest.

If you are really progressing through *dunya*, living and fulfilling these three different levels of the hadith of Prophet, then your password will be given to you. They gave you your password on *al-yawma alastu bi rabbikum qālū balaʿ*, on the Day of Promises when our Lord said, "Am I not your Lord?" and we said, "*Bala*—yes." Your password was released to you there, but you came to *dunya* and forgot it because of negative energy, or all the desires of this *dunya*, the dirty desires, that have veiled you since your childhood.

When you reached adulthood, it was with a blend of heavenly inspirations and desires of this dirty world. That made it impossible for you to remember that password. Sometimes if you forget your password, various sites will give you a hint to remember it. Allah ﷻ also gave you some hints to remember your password in *dunya*.

I will tell the story of Grandshaykh ق and Mawlana Shaykh Nazim ق to show you how it works. By order of Prophet ﷺ Grandshaykh ق was ordered to do seclusion for six months in Madinat al-Munawwarah in the same room with Mawlana Shaykh Nazim ق. Before that, a *Sultan al-Awliya* never kept his *mureed* with him in same room during seclusion because too many states or trances happen that the *mureed* cannot carry. But with his power, Grandshaykh ق was able to make sure that the young Mawlana Shaykh Nazim could carry that.

Your Password Opens Your Trust

Grandshaykh ق ordered Mawlana Shaykh Nazim to go daily to *Masjid an-Nabawi ash-Sharif* from *Madrassat al-Shoona* of the Bukhari people, who put that school to teach Holy Qur'an and *Shari`ah* under that name. That route took about fifteen minutes by foot. He was ordered that as soon as he stepped out from the building, one of the eleven principles of Shah Naqshband, *an-nazar bar qadam*, keep your eyes on your feet without looking right or left, as in seclusion to look elsewhere is forbidden. So five times a day he went along the way looking only at his feet, pray, and he returned the same way. Each time he went, he had to take *ghusl*, the ritual shower. He was permitted to sleep one or two hours in twenty-four hours. He may have completed one *khatm* of Holy Qur'an or more every day. To look only at one's footsteps and remain not attracted to anything around you, coming and going with *adab* is not easy.

So at last, he finished and was so happy. Even with all the deprivation and sacrifice of seclusion, you quickly forget that and say, "I want to go another time," because that intense *ishq*, the love of Allah ﷻ and Prophet ﷺ increases there.

So Mawlana Shaykh Nazim ق was returning from *Haram an-Nabi* and came out from *Bab al-Fatima*. The precise *adab* is to come to the holy presence of Prophet ﷺ from *Bab al-Jibrīl* and make *salam* to Prophet ﷺ, Sayyidina Abu Bakr ؓ and Sayyidina 'Umar ؓ.[2] Then you go to *Mahbit al-Wahi*, where Sayyidina Jibrīl ؑ used to descend, and pray two *raka`ats*. From there you go left to where Sayyida Fatima az-Zahra ؑ is buried,[3] and then to the grave reserved for Sayyidina 'Isa ؑ, and then you make *du'a*. Every time you enter *Haram an-Nabi* you have to do that. Then you go to the presence of Prophet ﷺ and ask permission to leave.

So when Mawlana Shaykh finished, he exited from *Bab al-Fatima* to where there used to be hills, a huge market and a residential area, and also a library of Arif Basha of Turkey, a famous Ottoman governor of Madinat al-Munawwara who ran the affairs of the city. Mawlana Shaykh passed that daily. I heard this story from Grandshaykh 'AbdAllah ق many, many times, but the last time he added these details:

> When Nazim Effendi was walking out and looking at his feet, I had asked the Prophet ﷺ, "*Ya Sayyidi, ya Rasulullah!* This is the last day of his seclusion. Can you certify that he is ready to receive his trust?" At that moment, I was on that high hill watching Nazim Effendi walk and I was standing between Sayyidina Muhammad ﷺ and Sayyidina Abu Bakr ؓ, to whom I turned and said, "*Ya Sayyidi!* Can you petition the Prophet ﷺ that my son is ready?" That is the *adab*. And that was

---

[2] Although they are not buried there, you must also give *salam* to Sayyidina 'Uthman (r), Sayyidina 'Ali (r), Sayyidina al-Hasan (r) and Sayyidina al-Husayn (r).

[3] Angels moved Sayyida Fatima ؑ near her father (s); people don't know that.

presented to Prophet ﷺ, who said to me, 'He is not ready yet. Don't give his trust.' At that moment, I knew the permission was not yet granted because Nazim Effendi didn't remember his password that was given to him on the Day of Promises, and first he must know it."

That is why *awliyaullah* say that every test has a very important password that, if you know it, opens your Trust from one door to another door. It was not yet ready, but why not? There is wisdom in that: Mawlana Shaykh Nazim was still on the road walking, and when he reached the room where they stayed he would get the last test. So Sayyidina Muhammad ﷺ, Sayyidina Abu Bakr ؓ and Grandshaykh ق observed Shaykh Nazim as he passed through all the roads, until he reached the school. To be under that observation is not easy. Allah ﷻ said in Holy Qur'an:

واعلموا أن فيكم رسول الله

W`alamū anna fīkum rasūlullah.
And know Allah's Messenger is in you. (Surat al-Hujurāt, 49:7)

Awliya can see you even if you are deep in a mine! So he entered the room and, Grandshaykh 'AbdAllah ق narrates:

I scolded him, "Why did you make me shy in front of the Prophet ﷺ? I presented you, and although you completed all your tests, Prophet ﷺ said you are still arrogant and that is why he didn't accept to give you your trust! Don't you know that Shaytan is the most arrogant? Why you are arrogant about your worshipping when I gave you six months of seclusion? I don't want to see you until I know why you are arrogant!"

Grandshaykh ق gave him a hard time, but he also gave him a hint to get his password.

All that time, Nazim Effendi was smiling at me. I said, "You are smiling? Go away from here!" Then he laughed and I said, "What, you're still here? Go from here!" Then I threw the plate on him. He said, "*Ya Sayyidi*! May I say the reason I am arrogant?" I said, "Yes, of course you have to say why are you arrogant." He said, "*Ya Sayyidi*, I have someone behind me who is like a roaring lion! I am proud because of you; you are my pride! I am depending on you and that is why I am proud, not of myself, but of being a student of such a great Shaykh!" At that moment, the Prophet ﷺ appeared and said, "Give him his trust."

Mawlana Shaykh's password was, "I have such a Shaykh like you," in one word. At that moment, more and more was passed to Mawlana Shaykh Nazim and he later became Sultan al-Awliya. Allah ﷻ gave everyone their password. Something has been given to you, but you have to know your password to get it!

So we go back to the 'Dome of Provisions.' Every *wali* has a dome and the greatest is the dome of Prophet ﷺ, which covers all of them from *al-`Arsh ar-Rahman* all the way down. Angels connect you, because you are connected to a shaykh that is connected to Prophet ﷺ, so you continuously receive spiritual provisions that are downloaded to your heart. At the same time you will receive the physical provisions you need in daily life. But remember, there is a password, so try to meditate on it; contemplate every day, because they will never give it to you easily and they want you to struggle to get it back.

Secrets of the Dome of Provisions

They are giving you hints. Every day after his *suhbat*, Mawlana Shaykh Nazim sings, *"dome dome, dome dome,"* which is why now they want to mention the Dome of Provisions and that password will come out at end of the series. We ask Allah to keep us under their guidance.

Angels were assigned to Prophet ﷺ that he uses however he likes. He assigns special angels to special people, reserved mostly for The Most Distinguished Naqshbandi Order. All other *tarīqahs* have angels that come to them from Prophet ﷺ, but in the *Naqshbandi Tarīqat* there are angels that no one except *Sultan al-Awliya* can see and describe.

As we mentioned at the beginning, Grandshaykh 'AbdAllah ق told us about the angels that are *muwakilīn* for the Prophet ﷺ, for worldly and heavenly provision. He said:

Not one of the 124,000 Prophets, no Messenger, no *wali* nor angel can reach the level of knowing the distinguishing characteristics of these angels. Only the Prophet ﷺ knows them because Allah ﷻ gave him these angels, and the inheritors of Prophet ﷺ who are *Sultans* of *awliya,* who have *Sultan adh-Dhikr* on their tongues can know these angels, and not every *Sultan al-Awliya* has *Sultan adh-Dhikr* on their tongue!

Later in this series, we will explain what is *Sultan adh-Dhikr*. Important secrets will come with this series, which they condensed and are now 'zooming in' to bring it out! Part 1 of the series is a stepping stone to Part 2, and we pray you will benefit and get these secrets.

Insha'Allah we will always be under the feet of Prophet ﷺ, Grandshaykh ق and Mawlana Shaykh ق, and under feet of Sayyidina Mahdi ؏! *Insha'Allah* we will see Prophet in *dunya* and *Ākhirah*.

May Allah ﷻ forgive us and may Allah ﷻ bless us.

Wa min Allahi 't-tawfīq, bi hurmati 'l-habīb, bi hurmati 'l-Fatihah.

And with Allah is success. For the sake of the Beloved, for his sake we recite the opening chapter of Holy Qur'an.

From Whom Can We Take Tariqah?

*A'ūdhu billāhi min ash-Shaytani 'r-rajīm. Bismillāhi' r-Raḥmāni 'r-Raḥīm.
Nawaytu 'l-arbā'īn, nawaytu 'l-'itikāf, nawaytu'l-khalwah, nawaytu 'l-'uzlah,
nawaytu 'r-riyāḍa, nawaytu 's-sulūk, lillāhi Ta'alā fī hādhā 'l-masjid.
Ati'ūllāha wa ati'ū 'r-Rasūla wa ūli 'l-amri minkum.
Obey Allah, obey the Prophet, and obey those in authority among you. (4:59)*

Those who are on authority are not easy people. They have something to depend on or no one will listen to them. If they are not supported it means they cannot keep their obedience, and cannot guide people to obedience and accepting them.

We see this in physical life: those in authority are supported to enforce the law or constitution that people must follow. So people are afraid of those on authority as they have something they can depend on, which is enforcing the law. But in spirituality, those on authority have different criteria or a different kind of support. First, they depend on whom they are taking their powers from and where and when they took it. Those are the *awliyaullah* ق who depend on the Prophet because they are his inheritors.

Sayyidina Abdul-Khāliq al-Ghujdawāni ق, one of the masters of the Golden Chain in Central Asia, was famous for doing *dhikr* deep in his well beside his school, which we saw when we visited Uzbekistan. From a thousand years ago they dug that well and until today it is running. He used to go down in the well and submerge himself in the water, do his *dhikr*, then quickly come up to breathe, then go down again and do his *dhikr*, in the summer and winter! In winter it is cold and even in summer it is cold because it is a well. He did that because *Shaytan* cannot be under water; water kills *Shaytan* because he is created from fire.

Fire moves quickly to eat everything. The only way to put fire down is whenever you see fire eating anything, trees or mountains or homes, the only thing stronger than fire is the supplication, *"Allahu Akbar, Allahu Akbar, Allahu Akbar,"* three times. Keep saying that and the fire will go down, because fire is anger. *Shaytan* is created from fire, and fire wants everything to itself. Similarly, anger wants everything to be only what it accepts. So putting anger down is like putting down fire. Say, *"Allahu Akbar* on my ego, *Allahu Akbar* on my bad behaviors,"* then it will drop down.

Awliyaullah know this wisdom, that nothing can put fire down except water, and nothing can put *Shaytan* down except water because *Shaytan* is created from *naar al-hasad*, the fire (anger) of jealousy, which is the head of every sin. As soon as you speak with someone and he gets angry, you cannot control him and he is lost! And if you speak with anyone today in a way that he doesn't agree with, he reacts with the fire of anger on you. That means there is no *taslimiyah*, submission to Allah ﷻ, and Islam is based on submission.

The Shaykh's Protective Shield

Tarīqah, which means "way" in Arabic, is the way *murīds* can put down their anger, so they can submit to the teachings of their teachers. Today the student wants to teach the teacher, whereas before, the teacher used to teach the student. Today if you have one-thousand students and one teacher, then you have a thousand "teachers" of the teacher! Now the teacher must submit to the student. He hopes by doing this, one day he will bring his students to the way of submission. The student will run, run, run away, but one day the teacher will bring him back. Then *Shaytan* enters and makes him run again!

It is always a struggle. Run, bring him back; run, bring him back. Then at the end if he doesn't bring him back he may send him a big test and, finished! So it's better not to take *baya'*. Why to be under that heavy burden? If you don't take *baya'* then you will be flying like a bird. But when you decide to take *baya'*, the master will give you a hard time. Like in old times in prison, they tied the prisoner's legs and whipped him until blood and pus came out from his wounds. Sins are like pus. The teacher wants to take them away, so he keeps beating where there is pus and you cry because of the pain, until you are clean.

The problem is, the Shaykh doesn't give you anesthesia. Doctors give you anesthesia so you don't feel it, but Shaykhs want you to feel it, to know how difficult the pain is when Azra'il, the Angel of Death, will come to take your soul, the trust. How much you will suffer from the pain of the soul coming out of the body!

So the discipline of the Shaykh will become very easy compared to the Angel of Death taking the soul of that person, which is very difficult. *Awliyaullah* have been dressed by the Prophet ﷺ in a heavenly dress of mercy, that permits them to be with their followers when their soul is taken, to make it so easy as they have already been disciplined by the Shaykh. Don't think when you take the hand of the Shaykh you will be suffering. In *dunya* you will suffer, but when you are leaving this *dunya* you will be very easy, comfortable and satisfied. We hope that when our soul is being taken away we will be in presence of our Prophet ﷺ and that it will be very easy!

Sayyidina Abdul-Khāliq al-Ghujdawāni ق did his *dhikr* under water so *Shaytan* cannot approach. *Shaytan* can approach anyone except Prophet ﷺ and the inheritors of the Prophet, and the house of *Shaytan* is in the heart.

> *Fa-waswasa lahuma ash-Shaytanu li-yubdiya lahuma mā wūriya 'anhuma min sawātihima wa qāla ma nahakuma rabbukuma 'an hādhihi ash-shajarati illa an takūna malakayni aw takūna mina al-khālidīn.*
>
> *Then Shaytan began to whisper suggestions to them, bringing openly before their minds all their shame that was hidden from them (before). He said, "Your Lord only forbade you this tree, unless you should become angels or such beings as live forever."* (Surat al-A'rāf, 7:20)

Shaytan whispered in the hearts of Sayyidina Adam ؏ and Sayyidatuna Hawā ؏. Sayyidina Adam is the father of human beings and a Prophet! Do you think *Shaytan* whispered to them but is not able to whisper to us? He can whisper at any moment. When he whispered to Sayyidina Adam, it was in order to show, as Allah ﷻ said in Holy Qur'an, that for one second Adam gave an ear to *Shaytan* and it made Adam naked. *li-yubdiya lahuma* ... to show them how they had been veiled. "*Sawātihima*" means their bad characters. "Private parts" is where problems come, so any bad behavior is also a private part to the soul. So as soon as *Shaytan* whispers and you give an ear, you are now naked and exposed to every negative energy, as you lost Allah's covering!

Like in an X-ray room, they close very thick lead doors as a shield, to prevent radiation from coming out. There is a spiritual shield that *awliyaullah* put on you that *Shaytan* cannot penetrate, as he has a fiery, damaging X-ray; as soon as he approaches you are finished. As soon as you accept what he says, in that moment the connection is made and your shield is removed. *Awliyaullah* know you need a shield at all times and they put it for you.

So Sayyidina Abdul-Khāliq al-Ghujdawāni ق did not want *Shaytan* to approach, he has a shield. But to get the spiritual shield you need to get the physical shield first, to protect you from *Shaytanic* whispering when you are doing *dhikr*. So he used to do *dhikr* under water as *Shaytan* cannot approach water. However, today we do our *dhikr* with *Shaytan*. We open the TV and do our *dhikr* while watching movies, programs, news, and we think we completed our *dhikr!* How are you going to shield yourself if Sayyidina Abdul-Khāliq al-Ghujdawāni ق was doing it in the well? Who is better: Sayyidina Abdul-Khāliq al-Ghujdawāni ق or us? But today because ignorance is so widespread, even if you do it while watching TV, still Allah ﷻ is happy with you.

Once, Sayyidina 'Abdur-Rahīm al-Māghribi ق, a famous Shaykh from Morocco in North Africa, visited Sayyidina Abdul-Khāliq al-Ghujdawāni ق in Central Asia. He came asking a question. Sayyidina Abdul-Khāliq al-Ghujdawāni ق carried the reality of "Ghawthiyya," the highest Station of Inheritance from the Prophet ﷺ and he was the *Sultan al-Awliya* of that time.

Once he heard a voice, "*Ya* Abdul-Khāliq! Go to that place and hit with your stick on that rock." Sayyidina Abdul-Khāliq al-Ghujdawāni ق heard that heavenly voice and thought, "What is the benefit to hit the rock with my stick?" And it came to him, "*Ya* Abdul-Khāliq! Go and submit, don't question!" He went and hit the rock with his stick, which showed him, "You have been inheriting from Sayyidina Musa ﷺ, who also hit the rock and the twelve springs came forth."

> *And remember Moses prayed for water for his people. We said, "Strike the rock with your staff," then gushed forth therefrom twelve springs. Each group knew its own place for water. So eat and drink of the sustenance provided by Allah, and do no evil nor mischief on the (face of the) earth.*
>
> (Surat al-Baqara, 2:60)

Hit the Rock of the Ego to Get Your Spiritual Provision

When Bani Isrā'īl were in a long drought and Allah ﷻ ordered Sayyidina Musa ﷺ to hit the rock, and then Allah gave his people provisions. That means when you need provision you need to hit a rock; that is the rock of the ego. So it means, "O Abdul-Khāliq! Go and hit on that rock as your followers are in need of the water coming out from it; it is of spiritual benefit." It means hit the rock in order for them to submit, and that will bring heavenly, spiritual provisions.

So he hit that rock and a spring came out from it, and he heard a voice saying, "*Ya* Abdul-Khāliq! From every drop of water coming out, I am creating an angel, and your duty is to give a name to each angel and every angel must have a different name and you cannot repeat any name." That means if there are ten-trillion angels, there must be ten-trillion unique names. Allah granted that great power to Sayyidina Abdul-Khāliq al-Ghujdawānī ق and the praise of those angels will be given to followers of the Most Distinguished Naqshbandi Order.

That spring is running until today, and Sayyidina Abdul-Khāliq al-Ghujdawānī ق is still naming those angels, and that *dhikr* they are making is still being written to the followers of the Naqshbandi Sufi Order. Don't think the Naqshbandi Order is like soccer game in progress! Behind it there are very important messages and issues that *awliyaullah* deal with for the benefit of their students.

We mentioned how much knowledge Allah ﷻ gave to Sayyidina Abdul-Khāliq al-Ghujdawānī ق to name each angel, but his responsibility also includes knowing how many praises each angel is doing and in what language, from the moment he is created up to Judgment Day. He also must assign each angel to a Naqshbandi follower, who receives the benefit of everything that angel does! And every angel has a unique assignment.

Shaykh ʿAbdur-Rahīm Māghribi ق came to Sayyidina Abdul-Khāliq al-Ghujdawānī ق asking him an important question about what everyone needs. Grandshaykh explains, he was one of the greatest *awliyaullah* of his time who studied with Sayyidina Khidr ؑ for nine years, studying *ʿIlm al-Hadith* and *ʿIlm at-Tafsīr al-Qurʾan*, the same *tafsīr* that Sayyidina Musa was trying to learn from Sayyidina Khidr. So someone of that caliber came to Sayyidina Abdul-Khāliq al-Ghujdawānī ق asking a question, and that indicates how much higher in knowledge he is.

When you want to learn to recite Holy Qurʿan, you cannot teach yourself; you can memorize it, but your recitation will not be correct until you learn from someone authorized to teach Holy Qurʿan, a *qāri*, as they know the proper pronunciations and intonations, the *tajwīd, tartīl,* and all the special rules of recitation, such as how each letter is recited, when to pause and when not to pause. They have been trained through a chain of reciters going all the way back to the *Sahābah*, who learned to recite Holy Qurʿan from Prophet ﷺ.

Similarly, in spiritual teachings you must take from someone who learned from his teacher all the way back to *Sahābah* and to Prophet. You cannot take *tarīqah* from just anyone; you must take from someone who already tasted from these realities, and he will put divine knowledge on your tongue and on your heart.

So Shaykh 'Abdur-Rahīm Māghribi ق asked, "From whom do you take *tarīqah*? Is it from the *wali* that can speak with deceased people from East to West?"

Sayyidina Abdul-Khāliq al-Ghujdawāni ق answered, "No."

Then he asked, "Is it the *wali* that knows about everything in this universe, and all that praises and glorifies Allah ﷻ from East and West? Can I take *tarīqah* from him? Can I study with him?"

And again Sayyidina Abdul-Khāliq al-Ghujdawāni ق answered, "No."

Then 'Abdur-Rahīm al-Māghribi ق didn't know what to say. If you cannot take from that *wali*, who then has the qualification to give him *tarīqah*? We are not speaking here of scholarly matters. In *tarīqah* there are some restrictions and the *wali* who has no right or authorization to teach keeps quiet. There are many hidden *awliya* that no one knows, so they keep quiet. What is the benefit of a *wali* teaching you and he can't take you to his level? That is why when Grandshaykh, may Allah bless him, was asked to take the responsibility for *tarīqah*, he said, "I don't want that responsibility."

His Shaykh, Shaykh Sharafuddin ق, said, "No one has been ordered to carry *tarīqah*. Why are you saying 'no'?"

Grandshaykh ق said, "What is the benefit, *ya Sayyidi*, if I cannot raise students to my level when they are sitting with me?"

So *awliyaullah* know the importance of giving *tarīqah*. I will quote in the end how it is bad to listen to someone who doesn't have the responsibility to teach *tarīqah*, as all his teaching will become negative on you because he is not qualified to give you *tarīqah*.

So then Shaykh 'Abdur-Rahīm Māghribi ق asked Sayyidina Abdul-Khāliq al-Ghujdawāni ق the third question, "Can I take or learn *tarīqah* from a *wali* that is able to reach from the below the Arsh and all the way down?" It means that *wali* he has achieved the ability to make *sajda* beneath the Throne of Allah ﷻ.

Sayyidina Abdul-Khāliq al-Ghujdawāni ق kept quiet, then he asked again, "*Ya Sayyīdī*, for Allah's Sake, can I take *tarīqah* from someone who is able to reach from under '*Arsh* level all the way down?"

Sayyidina Abdul-Khāliq al-Ghujdawāni ق looked again said, "No."

If this is "no," and this is "no," and this is "no," from whom he will take knowledge? It means whatever we are speaking is not yet from the right level to teach, which means you are not yet eligible to teach and those listening are not yet taking from the right side of *tarīqah*; they are taking from the name of the teachings but not taking the secret of it. *Awliya* try to get the secret from every word they are speaking, in order to pour it in your heart!

Then he asked, "What about the one who reached the universe and the Seven Heavens in a moment without moving from his place, and he can be everywhere Allah created? Can I learn from him and take *tarīqah*?"

What do you think Sayyidina Abdul-Khāliq ق said, yes or no? He said, "no!" So then, from whom can we take *tarīqah*?

Then Shaykh 'Abdur-Rahīm Māghribi ق asked Sayyidina Abdul-Khāliq al-Ghujdawāni ق, "Then to whom I am going to give myself? Who is that one?"

Before that point, he did not surrender himself. He posed questions in a way to show he knows something, asking, "Can I take *tarīqah* from the one who reaches deceased people, or from the one who knows the praises of all creation to Allah?" He was praising his ego there. When he asked, "Can I take from the one praising under the Throne?" he was showing he knows all these various levels of *awliya*. When Sayyidina Abdul-Khāliq ق told him "no," he gave up and finally he realized, "*Ya Sayyidi*, I don't know."

Through that lesson Sayyidina Abdul-Khāliq ق taught him, "Don't show knowledge in my presence." There are people that like to keep talking to show they know about everything in normal life or in spiritual life. We all try to say we know something. In normal life it is alright, but it is better to keep quiet in the presence of a *wali*. Don't talk! If you talk you will make a mistake and if you don't talk you are safe. People who give presentations like to show themselves; they don't surrender, but rather they run to get fame. If you ask *awliyaullah*, "Do you want to make a presentation or an interview?" they will decline because they don't like to speak unless they are forced.

Shaykh Ahmad al-Badawi and the Key

So Shaykh 'Abdur-Rahīm Māghribi ق asked, "What am I going to do now? I tried all my knowledge to find that point."

Like the incident with Shaykh Ahmad al-Badawi ق of Egypt, who asked, "Open Your door, *Ya Rabbī!*" and someone came and said, "I have your keys; surrender yourself to me."

Astonished, he answered, "Who am I to surrender to you?" To surrender to Allah ﷻ is acceptable to most people, but there is a discipline: first surrender to the teacher, then to the Prophet ﷺ, then to Allah ﷻ. So he replied, "I'll take the key from the Keymaker only!"

Then that one left and Ahmad al-Badawi ق heard voice, "Do you want your key? I left it with that *wali* whom you kicked away!"

Then he knew he must take from that one, but his ego came in the way. Sayyidina Ahmad al-Badawi ق was looking for that *wali*, running for six months, to teach him patience. Finally, that *wali* appeared in front of him.

Sayyidina Ahmad al-Badawi ق said, "O my brother! Where were you?"

That *wali* answered, "I was here, but you could not see me."

"Can I have my keys?"

"You are too late, my brother. When I came and offered, you refused. Now you want it, and now I will not give it; I need the price for it."

Sayyidina Ahmad al-Badawi ق said, "I will give whatever wealth I have, my home."

"We are not after your *dunya* wealth."

"What I have to give then?"

"I want your knowledge, all what you have been taught and what you learned from books and what you have done of worship, saying, 'I did this, I did this, I did this.' Always you were selfish and branding everything as from you. I want that selfishness, that selfish knowledge that you built your ego on."

Allah ﷻ said in Holy Qur'an:

Which then is best? He that lays his foundation on piety to Allah and His good pleasure, or He that lays his foundation on an undermined sand-cliff ready to crumble to pieces, and it does crumble to pieces with him, into the fire of Hell. And Allah guides not people that do wrong. (Surat at-Tawbah, 9:109)

On a cliff it will fall apart into Hellfire. It means you cannot build your knowledge on ego, because if you are in *tarīqah* your ego will be down sooner or later. So the *wali* told him, "I cannot let you have this knowledge." Ahmad al-Badawi ق was a Grand Mufti in Tanta, a famous area in Egypt, where two-million people visit his *maqām* annually.

That *wali* said, "Give me that knowledge."

Ahmad al-Badawi ق said, "Okay."

So he looked into that *wali's* eyes and the *wali* pulled everything out like a magnet pulling metal. He left Ahmad al-Badawi ق knowing nothing, not even one word, not even recitation of Surat al-*Fatihah*! When you make a mistake in recitation of Surat al-*Fatihah*, it means *awliya* are taking away that knowledge. So he pulled everything from Ahmad al-Badawi ق until he didn't know anything, until children teased him for being ignorant!

If you lose your mind, still you will be okay. Everyone around the world thinks he knows something. Look, when Mawlana Shaykh, may Allah give him long life, gives a daily speech on Sufilive.com, people are so happy to listen; they stop their work and stop everything just to listen. Why? Because his message is reaching their hearts and they are ready to receive that information. And everyone is so happy and praising Mawlana with high titles out of love, as they know without him they are nothing! So those watching are lucky. There are some not watching; if they have an excuse such as work, it's okay. But others are proud of themselves. Who do you think you are if you are not watching? Is Mawlana Shaykh wasting his time to broadcast? Give at least a half-hour from your *dunya* life to watch and listen; it is better.

So in any case, that *wali* took everything from Sayyidina Ahmad al-Badawi ق and left him for six months, and children were running after him, saying, "Our Grand Mufti became crazy!" And he was looking for that *wali,* looking and looking, and that *wali* hid himself again.

Then he appeared and said, "*Ya* Ahmad! Are you ready?"

He answered, "I am ready."

When You Submit to Your Shaykh

That was after long struggle. He had heard a voice saying, "Take the key from this one." Had he accepted from the beginning, he would have reached higher levels!

Even so, that *wali* said, "Look in to my eyes now," and he poured knowledge from his heart into Ahmad al-Badawi's eyes until he could not look anymore, until his eyes were like lightning! He opened the Six Realities of the Heart, about which we have spoken many times: the Reality of Attraction (*Haqiqatu 'l-Jazbah*); the Reality of Downpouring (*Haqiqatu 'l-Fayd*); the Reality of Focusing (*Haqiqatu 't-Tawajjuh*); the Reality of Intercession (Haqiqatu 't-Tawassul); the Reality of Guidance (*Haqiqatu 'l-Irshād*); and, the Reality of Scrolling (*Haqiqatu 't-Tayy*). From then on, whoever looked in Ahmad al-Badawi's eyes fainted. So he surrendered in the end.

'Abdur-Rahīm al-Māghribi ق understood that any question he asks, his Shaykh, Sayyidina Abdul-Khāliq al-Ghujdawāni ق, replied "no." He asked five questions and each one was rejected.

Then he said, "*Ya Sayyidi*, to whom I am going to surrender myself?"

Then he understood and he came to submission. Beyond that nothing can be achieved; if you don't surrender to the Shaykh's will you cannot get anywhere or achieve anything. For example, everyday Mawlana Shaykh is giving a lecture and many people are translating it into different languages, and if you listen, it is enough; if you understand or not, the secret is pouring into your heart! Like when the computer is uploading information, you see green bars indicating progress of the upload. If you text message a picture or attachment, you open it, and it goes slowly, slowly, then it opens, but the next time it immediately opens, it doesn't take time.

Similarly, Mawlana Shaykh is filling you with these lights; you might not understand it, but when the time comes to open, it is already there. You will be moved like a rocket to a level where they want to raise you. Now you might not be raised; you might hear a *suhbah* and forget it, but your heart doesn't forget it, and your heart has downloaded that information already. You download it and in one second you can check it and see it. When the time of downloading comes and the Shaykh gives you your key, it opens all these words of light, secrets of knowledge that he is speaking about, and you can see what level he is speaking from, where he is standing and saying greeting to Prophet and saying *shahādah*.

From where he is standing? Where? Is Mawlana Shaykh standing in Lefke, by his chair? When he is greeting Prophet, he is standing in the Divine Presence of Prophet! And when the time comes, you will see it, what you have heard and learned from him will appear as Realities.

That will appear when you surrender, but today we are not surrendering. You see people chatting even. Why they are chatting when Mawlana Shaykh is speaking? Chat before or after. When you surrender, then your computer is ready to receive all the infomation uploaded to your heart.

Shaykh 'Abdur-Rahīm al-Māghribi ق said, *madha afal,* "I am surrendering myself. What must I do? I need an answer. I am coming to you to surrender. Which *wali* do I have to surrender to?"

He is still making a mistake because he doesn't realize, "This is the *wali* who is responsible for you!" By asking, "Which *wali,*" it is better to be a shepherd of sheep. You are asking all these questions and he is repeatedly saying "no," and at the end he is still asking, "Which *wali*?" There are many people like that. Are you not happy with the *wali* you are speaking with?

In the end, Sayyidina Abdul-Khāliq al-Ghujdawāni ق asked Shaykh 'Abdur-Rahīm al-Māghribi ق and he surrendered, although his ego was not in complete submission. So he said, "O my master! From whom can we take *tarīqah*?"

As we explained previously, now he understood his knowledge was of no benefit and what he asked is not going to benefit him. So finally he had to submit to Abdul-Khāliq al-Ghujdawāni ق, and he said, "*Ya Sayyidi*! From where do we take *tarīqah*?"

Grandshaykh ق said, "*Tarīqah* can only be taken from that *wali* who was with you on the Day of Promises when Allah ﷻ asked the gathered souls, 'Who are you and Who am I?' Only that *wali* can take you to your promises, *'uhūd*, which you vowed to fulfill on that Day."

So as we explained before, there are four levels of guiding Shaykhs: Murshid at-Tabarruk, Murshid at-Tasfiyya, Murshid at-Tazkiyyah and Murshid at-Tarbiyyah. Murshid at-Tabbaruk cannot pour into your heart the realities of *tarīqah*, to understand secrets of everything Allah ﷻ created. So what is the benefit of taking *tarīqah* from such a Shaykh?

Wa man kāna fi hādhihi 'aama fa-huwa fi'l-ākhirati 'āma wa adallū sabīla.

For whoever is blind (of heart) in this (world) will be blind in the life to come (as well), and still farther astray from the path (of truth).

(Surat al-Isrā', 17:72)

You are not studying that. It means he is blind from finding the truth so he will be blind all the way; he is not going to taste honey, it might be he tastes sugar. It is still a taste, but it is sugar; there is a big difference between honey and sugar. Do you want sugar or honey?

So the *wali* that doesn't have these particulars cannot take his *murīd* to the goal, which is *ilahī anta maqsūdī wa ridāka matlūbī*, "You are my goal and I want You to be happy and satisfied with me."

Does Allah laugh? Yes or no? (yes.) Okay what is evidence? *Rai'atu rabbī dāhikan*. "I saw My Lord coming to me laughing." That is why when Mawlana asked Shaykh Tahir al-Qadri that, he said yes, because it has evidence in this *hadīth* of Prophet. If it didn't have evidence then there will be a question mark.

Does Allah cry, the opposite of laughing? Does He? No. Because there is no evidence that Allah cries, because no one can harm Him. Only Allah is smiling. So someone who is laughing and smiling, is Allah going to hate him? If Allah is not hating anyone, then what do you think will happen to people? They will be forgiven.

> Ya Muhammad! I gave you an ummah that does not tire from doing sins and I am their Lord; I never tire of forgiving them.

Do you like to watch dirty things? No one likes to watch something dirty, especially old people. May Allah give us health and Sayyidina Muhammad said, "O Allah! Save my *ummah* from the sudden death," because it is too heavy on the family and too heavy on the deceased. Prophet said, "The best death is the easy one and in the bed." O Allah! Give us that, with health, and when You want the soul of Your servant back, take it with the easiest way and simplest way!

So Allah doesn't harm. Allah is always happy. He looks at our goodness.

So Abdul-Khāliq al-Ghujdawāni, may Allah bless his soul, said to him, "The one who is in the Divine Presence has reached to be able to see all the way to the Day of Promises and see what everyone has promised Allah to do in *dunya*."

And Allah divided the whole crowd on *awliya*; each one took a group of people to clean them and return them clean, as they have been given to him. In the Divine Presence, everyone is clean with no dirtiness. When we came to *dunya* we became dirty. So that *wali* in the Divine Presence has been given authority to look into that, like the captain over his soldiers and he has to be responsible for those people under his control. The captain cannot allow one of his soldiers to be captured and if someone is captured, he will do his best to rescue him.

By authority of the Prophet and Allah given to him, a *wali* will not allow *Shaytan* to take any of his students. If he cannot reach that level it is better to step aside. For those who don't have that authority, it is better to tell their students, "I am like you. We are all under the banner of our Shaykh."

O human beings! O students of Mawlana Shaykh! Every time Mawlana sits to speak he says and admits, "I am a weak servant." How then do you claim you are a Shaykh? Yesterday he was saying that authority been given to the *qutb* that Allah is giving the last chance to people. If they are not going to repent, those who are not repenting are going to suffer. And this is a declaration coming to him from the *qutb*. He didn't say, "I am the *qutb*." He was able to say that. Why he didn't say it? There are two meanings here.

One is, he doesn't want his ego to claim anything. *Awliyaullah* know themselves. I am not going to explain about Mawlana Shaykh, but only to say he doesn't want to be proud of what has been given to him; he always wants to show humbleness. *Awliyaullah* inherit from the Prophet, who said, "I am only a human being like you." Prophet is showing humbleness.

Qul innama 'ana basharun mithlukum yuhā ilayya.
Say (Ya Muhammad!), 'I am only a servant like you, but I receive revelation."
(Surat al-Kahf, 18:110)

"*I receive revelation*" changes the whole subject, but square-minded, stupid people cannot understand it! Allah is instructing Prophet to say, "I am a human being, but I receive Divine Revelation." When you show humbleness, then Allah reveals to you. But in *yuhā ilayya*, "revealed to me," who is speaking to Prophet? Allah is speaking to him through His messenger, Jibrīl. So who can have this specialty? No one else! So *lā tansab li nafsika ayyi shay*, "Don't claim anything to yourself." If you claim, you lose. That is why *awliyaullah* always speak in the abstract, *damīr*, using the pronouns, "they," "he" or "she." They never say "I" as that is selfish, meaning, "me." "They" is the one sitting there. He said, "The *qutb* sent this declaration." Who is the *qutb*? Mawlana Shaykh Nazim is the *sultān* and the *qutb* is under him!

The second meaning is, he wants to tell those who understand that the order has passed from him to the *qutb*; the *sultān* gives the order and the *qutb* executes the order. That is why he referred it to the *qutb*, not to himself. So he said, "This is a heavenly declaration from the *qutb* declaring that."

There are five *qutbs*; which of them does he mean? He doesn't want to say "I," so he left it. The five *qutbs* are: *Qutb, Qutb al-Aqtab, Qutb al-Bilad, Qutb al-Irshad, Qutb al-Mutassarif*. For sure it is *Qutb al-Mutassarif*. He is the *ghawth* who receives the order from the Prophet ﷺ and passes the declaration to one of these *qutbs*, And he is completely hiding himself.

So *awliyaullah* don't like to expose themselves and say, "We did this or that." We have to be constantly aware of this, precisely how we can express ourselves as listeners. Those who are Shaykhs—or who have been considering themselves as Shaykhs, whoever they are—have to be very particular and precise in what they say. When Mawlana Shaykh says, "I am the weakest," it actually means, "I am highest." So if Mawlana Shaykh is weak, where are the rest? They are minus, less than zero! So if you are making yourself a Shaykh, you are responsible. It is better to be sheep, not the shepherd!

So 'Abdur-Rahīm al-Māghribi ق is coming to Sayyidina Abdul-Khāliq al-Ghujdawāni ق to be a Shaykh, and Abdul-Khāliq is telling him, "No, you don't know." 'Abdur-Rahīm is saying, "I know." If from the beginning he said, "I came to submit myself to the *wali* who can carry me," he would have made quick progress. Instead, he began to display different knowledges by asking different questions.

The Prophet never showed his knowledge. He was always waiting for *wahī* (revelation). Even with the story of Sayyida A'yesha ؓ (when she lost her necklace in the desert), he waited one month until revelation came informing the people, "She is the highest of ladies." So when you keep quiet and don't make noise, they are happy with you. When you want to show your knowledge. they are not happy with you. Therefore, *lā tansab ayyi shayin li nafsik*, "Do not attribute anything to yourself." Make your Shaykh happy with you.

Grandshaykh ق gave *suhbah* for one or two hours, speaking non-stop like a waterfall, and people got tired. When Mawlana Shaykh raised his hands in *du'a*, then Grandshaykh ق ended the *suhbah*.

When the Shaykh is finished speaking, make him happy. I used to see Mawlana Shaykh say to Grandshaykh when he finished, "Today *masha'Allah,* you put us in big oceans! We were diving in that ocean!" and Grandshaykh ق laughed and was so happy.

Today when he finishes the live broadcast, sometimes we are lucky to call him and say, "O Mawlana! Those were big oceans you put us in!"

He says, *"Masha'Allah,* what I said? Are people happy? How many people?"

"O Mawlana, one-million!"

"Okay, that is nice."

When you keep *awliyaullah* happy, Allah ﷻ is smiling. Allah doesn't like people grouchy, always looking serious and angry, He likes people very bright, laughing and smiling.

The Shaykh From Whom You May Take

So at the end Sayyidina Abdul-Khāliq al-Ghujdawāni ق explained the importance of knowing every detail about his *murīd* on the Day of Promises. That *wali* who knows every detail about what you promised, you can take *tarīqah* from him.

But it was as if 'Abdur-Rahīm al-Māghribi ق didn't understand anything and he kept asking, "Where I can find that one?"

He said, "O my son. You have been sitting with us for seven years." He spent nine years under Sayyidina Khidr's teaching and then seven more years with Sayyidina Abdul-Khāliq al-Ghujdawāni ق, and he didn't know who is that Shaykh! Scholars are arrogant and it is very difficult for them to submit. The four enemies inside you, *nafs, dunya, hawa, Shaytan,* cause the ego, desires, and love of this world to play with you. That is why it is very difficult to submit. That is how *Shaytan* enters between a husband and wife, to create *fitna* and divide them.

So he said, "You are sitting seven years in this house, but if you want to find who is that man, when people come here observe to whom they are connected." So he didn't submit and he was waiting to see to whom the people connect. The *murīds* came and they said, *"Ya Sayyidi,* the circle is completed. We need to renew our *baya'* with you." Then he understood that Sayyidina Abdul-Khāliq al-Ghujdawāni ق was that one.

When you find that one you find the fruit. Then he took initiation and with the *suhbah,* his Shaykh made him ready and took him all the way, to know what is his daily duty by looking at the Preserved Tablet.

That is why Grandshaykh ق said, in the time of Sayyidina al-Mahdi ﷺ he will connect everyone to the Preserved Tablet and we will know the Standard Operating Procedures, SOPs, written in the Preserved Tablet. Everyone will see their daily responsibilities.

Sahābah used to take from the Prophet directly. *Mureeds* have to connect through their *shuyukh* who have permission to look at the Preserved Tablet and who connect to their *murīds* to get their Standard Operating Procedures, which they follow.

Also, *awliyaullah* who have been ordered to do so go from east to west to look for people, to support them and to give them *suhbah* and lectures to train them. As they will be far from their *shuyukh,* they have authority to connect the people to their Shaykh, which is Mawlana Shaykh, and then they will be able to follow their SOPs.

Sayyidina 'Abdur-Rahīm al-Māghribi ق was granted that. Then he was authorized by his Shaykh to teach, and he reached the level of *musta'id,* Prepared. So he was not even a Shaykh yet, he was a *murīd.* We call everyone *murīds,* but really they are at the level of lovers, not *murīds*; *insha'Allah* we will be true *murīds* one day.

This is very important. He said, "If someone has been chosen to be student of certain a *wali* who has knowledge of what happened in the Divine Presence, but that *murīd* went to another *wali,* even if that *wali* has authority from the Divine Presence and he knows what happened there, if he taught that *murīd* anything, that teaching will become negative on that *murīd.*"

That *murīd* must take from his own Shaykh, not from the step-Shaykh who in Islam is like a stepfather. That is a big problem people fall into. There are too many so-called Shaykhs and the people are losing their connection by taking *baya'* with them and forgetting about their original spiritual father, Mawlana Shaykh Nazim ق. If they have been told that the real one is that one, then it is okay (they are innocent), but even if the other one is a *wali,* you cannot go to someone who doesn't carry your responsibility.

One example of this is when Mawlana Shaykh Nazim ق was young and studying in Istanbul, he left and went traveling in Allah's Way. He used to frequent Sultan Ahmad Mosque, a very big mosque, the Blue Mosque, near Topkapi Palace of the Ottomans. There he would see Shaykh Jamaluddin al-Alusī and say to him, "I want to take initiation."

But Shaykh Jamaluddin said, "I am not carrying the responsibility of your share in the Divine Presence. Your Shaykh is not here, he is in Damascus, so go there." He didn't say, "Come! I will give you initiation."

It was the WWII and there were terrible bombings and danger but despite that, he went there. True *wali*s know whose *murīd* is whose and they avoid the responsibility to take the *murīd* of another Shaykh as that is cheating. Murshid at-Tabarruk, Murshid at-Tasfiyyah and Murshid at-Tazkiyyah may still have some traces of ego and may like to take more students, but in doing so they are not fulfilling their responsibility.

Mawlana Shaykh ق went all the way to Damascus and came to Midan Square where he met Grandshaykh, may Allah bless his soul. That story is in *The Naqshbandi Sufi Way* and you can read it there. *Taqabal-Allah.*

May Allah ﷻ forgive us and may Allah ﷻ bless us.

Wa min Allahi 't-tawfīq, bi hurmati 'l-habīb, bi hurmati 'l-Fatihah.

And with Allah is success. For the sake of the Beloved, for his sake we recite the opening chapter of Holy Qur'an.

The Threat of an Eloquent Hypocrite

*A'ūdhu billāhi min ash-Shaytani 'r-rajīm. Bismillāhi' r-Rahmāni 'r-Rahīm.
Nawaytu 'l-arbā'īn, nawaytu 'l-'itikāf, nawaytu'l-khalwah, nawaytu 'l-'uzlah,
nawaytu 'r-riyada, nawaytu 's-sulūk, lillāhi Ta'alā fī hādhā 'l-masjid.
Ati'ūllāha wa ati'ū 'r-Rasūla wa ūli 'l-amri minkum.
Obey Allah, obey the Prophet, and obey those in authority among you. (4:59)*

It is surprising to still see people interested in accepting these kinds of gatherings; even with 24-hour entertainment and temptations, people leave their homes and spend time in such gatherings. It is a proof of piety and sincerity still within human beings, especially when parents bring their children, because they will raise them on an environment that is very loved by Sayyidina Muhammad.

Human nature always wants to go astray; it does not like to sit and follow the footsteps of Sayyidina Muhammad ﷺ. Those who are not happy with such gatherings, you will find them on the other side. So my master, may Allah give him long life, Sayyidi Shaykh Muhammad Nazim Adil al-Haqqani, is very happy when he sees such groups around the world remembering Allah ﷻ and Sayyidina Muhammad ﷺ. Especially those whom, although they are Muslim, were not raised to be dedicated to Islam and especially those who were not Muslim but who were guided to Islam. And also Mawlana Shaykh is happy with those not raised as real (practicing) Muslims but were "Muslims" by name only, and they accepted to come and attend and worship as best as they can. Allah ﷻ is happy with them and Prophet ﷺ is happy with them and their rewards cannot be described!

The Nature of Hypocrites

No one really knows the hearts, except Allah ﷻ. He gave His Prophet, Sayyidina Muhammad ﷺ that knowledge, and Prophet gave *awliyaullah* that knowledge to see what is in the hearts of people. Everyone knows what is in his heart, *i.e.*, what he likes or what he is planning, but no one knows it except that person alone and also the teacher (Shaykh, *murshid*) who receives permission from Prophet ﷺ to read hearts. We have to know that Allah and Prophet ﷺ are seeing us by Allah's authority and order, and *awliyaullah* are seeing us by Prophet's order. The Shaykh can see and hear his *murīd*; every movement comes to his ears like thunder.

'Ilm al-Qulūb, Knowledge of Hearts, is for *awliyaullah*. That is why *munafiqūn*, hypocrites, think what is in their hearts is hidden, as Allah ﷻ describes in Holy Qur'an. That is why they say things to please you while their hearts are completely against you. If they did that to Sayyidina Muhammad ﷺ, as we know from the many verses Allah ﷻ revealed about them, what do you think in such an environment like today? Are they going to sit still or step up their projects, programs, plots and plans?

Munafiqūn always use Allah's message to reach their goals, which are completely different than what they say. If you compare teachings of a so-called *wali* to teachings of a real *wali*, you will find a great difference. One wants to express his knowledge and dazzle people with highly academic presentations, and the other uses very simple language and a humble presentation that strikes the heart like an arrow! That is a real *wali*, and you can notice that by how they speak. When the so-called *wali* or scholar speaks, you see their arrogance and how they feel about themselves because they are show-offs. So next time when you are on Sufilive.com listening to Mawlana Shaykh Nazim ق, try to focus on the way he speaks. You can see him waiting for inspiration to come to his heart to speak. It is not like a scholar who gives different statements from books he memorized.

I will tell you frankly that since I knew Mawlana Shaykh Nazim ق, I never saw him memorize anything. His heart is directly connected to Prophet ﷺ so he speaks spontaneously and his words are like missiles. If you don't feel it, your heart will feel it.

Sufilive.com viewership is increasing; we are now rated the fourth channel of the top one-thousand channels on Livestream.com (global rating)! Hundreds of thousands of people are listening every 24 hours. We don't know where they are from; we know some of them, some we cannot know. Why? Because words are like rockets of *nūr*, heavenly Light that reaches people's hearts and pulls them to the broadcasts.

Similarly, on a small scale, in every country there are many different locations for Mawlana Shaykh's students who listen and gather, and they are blessed to be together under the banner of a *wali* considered *Sultan al-Awliya*! We consider our Shaykh as *Sultan al-Awliya*, and I don't want to criticize others who might call their Shaykh "*Sultan al-Awliya*," but we have to be very careful about whom we listen to and from whom we take in all these different locations around the world. We must know about who is really dedicated to Mawlana's love and who is not. I can say that most of them but not all of them are for sure dedicated to love of Mawlana, or else why make a location if they have no love to the Shaykh? In our *tarīqah* and in many other *tarīqahs* it is the same. But you have to be careful for the handful that use the name of the Shaykh solely for their personal benefit and advantage, because one rotten apple in the basket will quickly contaminate the whole basket of apples.

Generally speaking, in the Naqshbandi Tarīqah or in other *tarīqahs* where such problems exist, they existed also in the time of Prophet ﷺ. Some hypocrites mingled among the *Sahābah* ؓ and they tried to disturb and contaminate the *Sahābah* with their rotten ideas by using the Names of Allah ﷻ and His Prophet ﷺ, when in reality they were against Allah and His Prophet! Allah ﷻ has asked us to avoid them and be very cautious regarding them.

Today people might ask, "Why are you wasting your time, energy and money to travel long distances just to be with your Shaykh?" This question may come to your heart also, as *Shaytan* is a big hypocrite and might inspire it. But in doing so, and by stepping over your *Shaytan* and coming here, you are not coming to the one who is speaking, you are coming to the original one to whom you intended. Further, you are coming because of your love of Mawlana Shaykh Nazim ق and you will be rewarded as if you travelled all the way to him in Cyprus! The time you spend here (in Michigan) is as if you went all the way to his place and spent the time there, because his secret is making us speak.

From Grandshaykh 'AbdAllah ad-Daghestani's ق generosity and love for us—may we always love him!—he often spoke of the importance of the *halaqah* circle and associations under someone authorized to speak on their behalf. He gave Mawlana Shaykh Nazim ق two helpers to spread that message under his name. This *majlis* (holy gathering) is getting its *barakah* from Mawlana Shaykh Nazim ق and from Grandshaykh ق, all the way to Prophet ﷺ! So it is not a waste of time and is considered complete worshipness during the entire time you are here or visiting Mawlana Shaykh in Cyprus.

It is written for everyone visiting, everyone staying, every moment of travel and being here, and it is rewarded, not only sitting in the *suhbah*, but in staying here or wherever, you will be rewarded for every second as if you are in full worshipness! Therefore, we have to be very careful from some bad apples that might contaminate the good apples, and I am speaking in general. As Prophet ﷺ said, you have to be very careful from the *munāfiq*, *'alīmun bi 'l-lisān jahūlan bi 'l-qalb,* "The one eloquent in speech but ignorant in his heart." He might divert you to somewhere else, where you lose both your way and your destiny!

The Real Wali Gives to You from the Heart of the Prophet

So try to focus on the next lecture of Mawlana Shaykh Nazim ق and check the way he speaks with very simple language while conveying priceless knowledge. When you look very carefully, you can trace the connection like tracing an email to the sender's IP address, to see where it came from. If you focus carefully, you find it goes all the way to Prophet ﷺ, and like a magnet, Mawlana Shaykh ق is taking and giving fresh from Prophet's heart!

If you look at someone else, you cannot trace his signal because his IP address is his own ego and it doesn't go any further. But if you trace Mawlana Shaykh's IP address there is no ego, and you can feel the presence of Prophet ﷺ in his speech! That is why it is important to listen to his speech. Just now, this moment is inspired by Mawlana Shaykh for me to say it. Encourage others to listen to the broadcast; listen to the main station, which is the station of Prophet ﷺ!

When Allah ﷻ revealed Holy Qur'an to Prophet, did anyone hear it? Only Prophet ﷺ heard that Heavenly Voice, and *Sahābah* ؓ were the only ones to hear Prophet's holy voice. Everyone else heard the Holy Qur'an either from *Sahābah* or from *imams* who came after them up to today. That is why if you are not connected with the main station, the way of reading the Qur'an is not perfect. *Awliyaullah* are able to listen through their lineage (*silsalah*) directly to what Prophet ﷺ, the main source, is telling them. It is a direct connection; you hear it in the sound of your Shaykh, but he is hearing directly from the heart of Prophet ﷺ. So there is no one between you and Prophet ﷺ except one! It is coming so strong because you are hearing it directly.

However, if you listen to other scholars, their teachings come from books. As we said yesterday, what benefit is in memorizing books and not practicing the knowledge? So it is big difference when you are getting a direct connection; that is enough for you in *dunya* and *Ākhirah*!

It is as we believe, coming on the tongue of the Shaykh from Prophet ﷺ, carrying immense light, mercy and blessings that Prophet disseminates to *awliyaullah*. What do you think if you are getting that from the head of *awliyaullah?* There is no one who will block you! Your Shaykh is there to unblock whatever is blocked! That is why it is important to listen when Mawlana Shaykh ق speaks. When he stands during the *suhbah*, at that moment he is in the Divine Presence, asking Prophet ﷺ to make that a fruitful association. Some scholars might not have even have *wudū* when they give a presentation. Mawlana Shaykh ق stands with respect when he mentions Prophet ﷺ. In one *suhbah* he stood twenty times because the presence of Prophet ﷺ was so immense!

On Sufilive.com, see how those sitting there with Mawlana Shaykh Nazim ق are honored by that presence and manifestation of mercy and blessing that descends! It is not only for those present with Mawlana Shaykh in that *suhbah* to be rewarded that he got from Prophet ﷺ when he petitioned, "*Ya Sayyidi, Ya Rasūlullah*! Let those sitting with me and those who are watching receive the same level!" Any such gathering, even watching online, is getting blessing as if you are there visiting him, and anyone visiting, that *wali* is obliged and responsible to take him to visit the Prophet ﷺ, as Prophet said, *man zāra qabrī wajabat lahū shafaʿatī*, "Whoever visits my grave will get my *shafaʿā* (intercession)."

Awliyaullah take their followers to visit Prophet ﷺ in his presence, and Prophet gives them his *shafaʿā* and brings them with him in Paradise! All these rewards are there, but we have to be careful from bad apples that might contaminate us and make problems. We are weak. We don't deserve anything except beatings! We are garbage. We are donkeys; not you, I am a donkey, the rest you are horses!

> *And be moderate in your pace and lower your voice, for the harshest of sounds without doubt is the braying of the ass.* (Surat al-Luqman, 31:19)

The most disgusting sound of creatures Allah ﷻ created is the braying of the donkey. It means 'donkeyness', ignorance, is our characteristic. We are ignorant, so we must open our eyes. Even Prophet ﷺ was worried from these bad apples. In a famous *hadīth*, he said:

Akhwafu ma akhāfu ʿala ummatī munāfiq ʿalīmu 'l-lisan.
What I fear most for my ummah is a hypocrite with an eloquent tongue.

You see many study *Shari'ah* and they are not Muslim; they teach it and they are bad apples. A university professor who teaches Islam but does not practice Islam is a *munāfiq*, a bad apple. Anytime you sit in his presence and listen to him, your heart is filled with darkness because his entire association is darkness. That one is not fit to be in a place except where they spit on him! Those who are professors and teachers of Islam and don't practice Islam are the worst as they are contaminating the whole education system. Today mostly secular people teach Islam.

Prophet ﷺ said, "I fear most for my *ummah* the eloquent hypocrite who has no light but only darkness in his heart and *Shaytan* is with him."

You can compare: when Mawlana Shaykh ق says something you feel he is connected with Prophet ﷺ, and others are connected with their ego. Prophet ﷺ is worried, so should we not be worried, as well? We have to open our eyes. There are people who don't know *Shari'ah* and *tarīqah*, but *nasabū li anfusikūm*, "They gave themselves a position to guide students." They are guiding people to a deep valley where wolves devour them at any moment! So we have to be very careful of that *munāfiq* who speaks well.

Such gatherings and meetings for the love of Mawlana Shaykh Nazim ق, from the time the person came until he goes is considered full worshipness: his eating, sleeping, every act, because he came for Allah and went for Allah!

Your Spiritual Blueprint

Prophet ﷺ said, (in many different narrations from Bukhari, most of them in authentic *ahadīth*):

وعن أبي عبد الرحمن عبد الله بن مسعود -رضي الله عنه- قال حدثنا رسول الله -صلى الله عليه وسلم- وهو الصادق المصدوق: إن أحدكم يُجمع خلقه في بطن أمه أربعين يومًا نطفة، ثم يكون علقة مثل ذلك، ثم يكون مضغة مثل ذلك، ثم يرسل إليه الملك فينفخ فيه الروح، ويؤمر بأربع كلمات: بكتب رزقه، وأجله، وعمله، وشقي أو سعيد، فوالله الذي لا إله إلا غيره إن أحدكم ليعمل بعمل أهل الجنة حتى ما يكون بينه وبينها إلا ذراع فيسبق عليه الكتاب فيعمل بعمل أهل النار فيدخلها، وإن أحدكم ليعمل بعمل أهل النار حتى ما يكون بينه وبينها إلا ذراع فيسبق عليه الكتاب فيعمل بعمل أهل الجنة فيدخلها رواه البخاري ومسلم

A child's formation in the womb of his mother begins to take shape within forty days, and then in another forty days it will be in a different cycle, then he will be a clot hanging in the womb of the mother, and then after his formation

he will become bigger, then Allah sends him an angel and that angel will give him four words. That angel has to send the soul to the body of the child. That angel blows the soul in him. The angel will be told (by Allah), "Write what he will do in dunya, that I already know (but) write it, as I want it to be a witness in Judgment Day."

Does Allah ﷻ need a witness, or can you speak there? All Prophets ﷺ and their nations are shaking on that Day, worried and afraid of what Allah is going to ask them! That is why they come to Sayyidina Muhammad ﷺ, to seek his intercession.

All your deeds in *dunya* are already known; they are in your blueprint. When Allah ﷻ through His will created you from His Beautiful Name, al-Khāliq, "The Creator," immediately the plan came from His Beautiful Name, al-Qādir, "The Powerful," and like huge building constructed of every single moment of your life, already your blueprint was written. So they already know what you are going to do, even how many hairs are in your beard! You and I don't know. If we don't even know that, what do we know from our inner self, if we know nothing from our outer self?

O *ghulam, murīd*, student! O servant of Allah! "Why are you claiming knowledge when you don't know the number of hairs in your beard?" That is the example Allah gave to measure your knowledge of self. No one can count the hairs on his head or the cells in his body. That angel knows, and that Divine Voice says, "Write the action of that servant!" And as soon as that voice comes it is written in a moment, and Prophet ﷺ said, *uktub 'amalahu,* and in one instant it is written! And that is so fast, and that angel will be always with that person until he leaves *dunya*.

And then the Voice will say, *wa rizqahu*, "Write whatever provision he will get," whatever you eat or drink or whatever money or wealth you get, in one instant it is written; with no thinking it is there.

Allah ﷻ says it, Prophet ﷺ is describing it to us. *wa ajalahu*, "And write the day of his death, the moment, measured in breaths." How many breaths you breathe in and out is your *ajal* in *dunya*, not how many days you have lived. The moment you can no longer breathe, that is death.

Then the Voice will say, *shaqī'in aw sa'īd*, "Write if he will be from gangs (punished people) or from the happiest people." Will they be from

Hellfire or from Paradise? Why in *ahadīth* sometimes the word *shaqī*, "gangs" appears before "good person." Even in Holy Qur'an, Allah ﷻ says:

> *Fa alhamaha fujūraha wa taqwaha.*
> *He inspired the self of its good and its bad.* (Surat ash-Shams, 91:8)

Allah ﷻ wants *khatimat al-umūr*, everyone's end, to be good! That is why "*shaqī*" is written first and "*sa'īd*" follows, because the bad will be down and the good rising up. That is all written: his *'amal*, his *rizq*, his day of death, and if at death he will be with bad or good people. That is all done in seconds, "*Kun!*" (Allah said "Be" and it is!) Before the *nun* enters the *kaf*, it happens.

Yanfukhu fīhi ar-rūh, "Then the angel blows the soul in him," then the child begins to move in the womb of the mother. All these issues have been uploaded to the child in its DNA. Scientists say DNA holds what is in your body, but in fact, all that you will do in *dunya* is written in your DNA after these plans are uploaded to that chip in your mind.

Some children die in the womb because their angel did not complete these four issues, or one of the four is not complete. Some die in the womb; others are born disabled. Only the child who has all four written is in perfect shape and the soul reaches him immediately.

You might be very dedicated all your life and then at any moment you decide to do something very bad, which takes you to the other side and in the end you go to Hell. They asked a very pious, sincere servant, "Did you see your Lord?" He answered, "If I did not see Him, I would have been cut to pieces." It means seeing not with vision, but seeing with *tawhīd*, belief in Divine Oneness. At this level, the heart is always in remembrance of the Creator.

Why the Live Broadcast Is Delayed

We will stop here, but I encourage people to watch Mawlana Shaykh Nazim on Sufilive.com. If they miss the live broadcast they can watch the recording, but to watch live is better and the other is like a photocopy, but still you get the blessings. The moment the live broadcast begins, the tap is open, the pipe from Prophet ﷺ to Mawlana Shaykh ق is open and he will take you to that holy presence. But when you see it later, that pipe is not open; then you are in the presence of the Shaykh, but not in the presence of Prophet.

Sometimes they ask why Mawlana Shaykh is delayed. Is Prophet ﷺ not on time? In that moment that pipe is in the heavenly environment, in the presence of Prophet ﷺ and you will be dressed with it. That is why those sitting there in the association with Mawlana Shaykh get that *tajalli*. So he petitioned Prophet ﷺ, "Let everyone watching me also receive that *tajalli*."

Timing is important, as Mawlana's tap is always open, but there is no permission to open it to others until a very precise moment, so sometimes he delays the broadcast. When he begins, the tap of divine energy from Sayyidina Muhammad ﷺ to Mawlana Shaykh is open to others.

May Allah give him long life and grant us long life to be with him to see Sayyidina Mahdi ؑ and Sayyidina 'Isa ؑ! And with that little bit, we are drowned from Mawlana Shaykh's ocean!

May Allah ﷻ forgive us and may Allah ﷻ bless us.

Wa min Allahi 't-tawfiq, bi hurmati 'l-habīb, bi hurmati 'l-Fatihah.

And with Allah is success. For the sake of the Beloved, for his sake we recite the opening chapter of Holy Qur'an.

੩੪ ੭

Benefits of the Halaqah (Dhikr Circle)

*A'ūdhu billāhi min ash-Shaytani 'r-rajīm. Bismillāhi' r-Raḥmāni 'r-Raḥīm.
Nawaytu 'l-arbā'īn, nawaytu 'l-'itikāf, nawaytu'l-khalwah, nawaytu 'l-'uzlah,
nawaytu 'r-riyaḍa, nawaytu 's-sulūk, lillāhi Ta'alā fī hādhā 'l-masjid.
Ati'ūllāha wa ati'ū 'r-Rasūla wa ūli 'l-amri minkum.
Obey Allah, obey the Prophet, and obey those in authority among you. (4:59)*

Allah ﷻ gave Prophet Muhammad ﷺ revelation. Only Prophets receive *wahī*, revelation, while others receive *ilham*, inspiration. Some Prophets received got *wahī*, which means they are also Messengers. And always the best is the last. You keep the best one for the cream, if you have a conference you leave the keynote speaker to the end to keep the people staying, not running.

Allah ﷻ did not only keep Sayyidina Muhammad ﷺ to be the Last Prophet (only) but He made him the First to be created and the last to be sent.

He ﷺ was the first in creation, which we know from when he was asked, "What was created first?" and he said, "*Ya* Jabir! The first thing Allah created was the Light of Muhammad."

And when Adam was between clay and water and still not yet formed, Prophet Muhammad ﷺ was already a prophet.

Prophet ﷺ is "as-Ṣādiq," Who Always Speaks the Truth, as well as "al-Masdūq," the Trustworthy One. From his birth until he left *dunya*, he was the only prophet whose name Allah ﷻ raised with His Name. You cannot raise anyone's name beside your name unless he is carrying your light or your name. Dressed by Allah ﷻ, Sayyidina Muhammad ﷺ carries the Ninety-Nine Beautiful Names and Attributes because there is no one above him or near him. He ﷺ is the only one in the Divine Presence with Allah ﷻ.

I was listening to *Sultan al-Awliya*, Mawlana Shaykh Nazim, may Allah give him long life, who said something we need to examine and understand. He said, "We say the Prophet ﷺ reached Qāba Qawsayni aw Adna, "The Station of Two Bows' Length or Nearer," so near Allah's Presence! We have to understand that although it is so near, that Presence is still out of the realm of Allah's Reality, His Essence. No one can be near His Essence."

"Presence" means you can be so close but still it is His Divine Presence, not His Essence, which is completely out of the Ninety-Nine Divine Names and the Divine Presence. Let us explain. In *dunya*, you can feel the presence of a king everywhere by the different projects he completed, but you cannot be with that king. Anything around you can show the presence of his touch. Mawlana Shaykh ق said, "The Prophet ﷺ reached the Divine Presence, but not *wujudiyyah ma' wujūd Allah 'Azza wa Jall*. There is no presence with Allah ﷻ; you cannot be present in His Essence, but everything around the Divine Presence can indicate His touch.

This shows the big misunderstanding people have today when they say, "My Shaykh is always with Allah ﷻ." No one can be there, not even if he worships day and night; he can be in the Divine Presence but not in the Essence Presence, Dhāt al-Buht, "the Unique Reality That Can Never Be Revealed." In fact, the most we know about Allah ﷻ is revealed through the Ninety-Nine Beautiful Names and Attributes.

Awliyaullah can be in the presence of the Prophet ﷺ in his association, but not in his reality. May Allah ﷻ always keep us in the presence of Sayyidina Muhammad ﷺ! Yes, they are his inheritors and they are servants of Allah. They can be with Prophet ﷺ, but not alone with Allah ﷻ in the Divine Presence. They must be with Prophet ﷺ as no one can enter the Divine Presence without the Prophet ﷺ, and even he cannot be with the Divine Essence ﷻ. As much as he is near, it is still the Divine Presence, not the Essence.

The Holy Qur'an was revealed to the Prophet ﷺ in this month. *Awliyaullah* inherit from these stunning knowledges and share some of it with their students, such as *fadīlat al-halaqah*, the reward or importance of the circle. Why is it *halaqah*, "a circle"; why not rows? Because every circle has a center, which is its significance, as energy radiates from the center through the circumference, so at equal distance it reaches everyone, whereas in rows you are not the center.

Your Qiblah Is Your Shaykh

Allah ﷻ gave us an indication that a center and the *halaqah*, circle, is important and the example is the *Ka'bah*. Wherever you pray there, the prayer lines around the *Ka'bah* form concentric circles; they are not lines but rather circles, with all devotees facing the center.

One cannot be a *wali* if he is not inheriting manifestations of whatever is manifested on Allah's House, the *Ka'bah*. In other words, if a *wali* cannot dress his students from those heavenly manifestations, he cannot be authorized as a *wali*, as *qiblatuka waliyuka*, "Your *qiblah* is your *wali*." Therefore, our central point that we have to look at is *awliyaullah*. In Sufism, the focus is your teacher, as when you pray your focus is Allah's House. In association, the Shaykh has to be your focus as he inherits the manifestation that comes on *Ka'bah*. How much he inherits depends on the *wali*. He is the focal point for everyone to understand and learn from him.

An example is, when you pray you focus your eyes on the point of *sajda*. In Mecca, when you pray in Masjid al-Ḥarām, you don't look at the point of *sajda*, you are ordered to look at the *Ka'bah*, the House of Allah ﷻ. *Awliyaullah* say looking at the *Ka'bah* is better than looking at forty *awliya*. When *awliyaullah* pray, they are in front of *Ka'bah*. When we pray, we only see where to make *sajda*, or we see the prayer carpet or the floor. That is why when some people pray, their eyes wander right and left, which means their prayer is wandering away from them!

Grandshaykh ق said, "When we go to *Ka'bah* to perform *Hajj*, *'Umra*, or to make *salat*, we must first give *salam* to *Ka'bah* by saying, "*As-salamu 'alayki ya Ka'abatullah! As-salamu 'alayk ya Hajar al-Aswad! As-salamu 'alayka ya Baytullah!*" *awliyaullah* hear the response, "*wa 'alaykum as-salam, ya 'AbdAllah*." That *salam* is from the House of Allah and from Hajar al-Aswad, the Black Stone! Grandshaykh ق said, "*Salam* from *Ka'bah* is not like *salam* from you and me. Even if you don't hear it, *awliyaullah* hear it, but you have to give *salam* whether you hear it or not. *Ka'bah* will answer your *salam* from the heavens, carrying with it all the power of Paradise, from Bayt al-Ma'mūr in the Fourth Heaven, which is the heavenly *Ka'bah* where Prophet ﷺ went in *Isrā' wal Mi'rāj*, and where he prayed on *Laylat al-Qadr*."

That means you have already been put in the Fourth Heaven; your first step in Heaven is established! That is why *Hajj*, the fifth pillar of Islam, is important, not because you go up and down from Mecca to 'Arafat, but because there are secrets carried along all the way, throughout all the rites of *Hajj*. One of those secrets is what we just said, that Allah ﷻ wants to give those who go for *Hajj* or *'Umra* or to pray there their first step in Heaven.

Allah's Mercy is huge! That is why it is a *fard* obligation to speak with *Ka'bah* and say, "*As-salamu 'alayki ya Ka'batullah!*" Some people ask, "Why speak to *Ka'bah* when it doesn't speak to you?" When Sayyidina 'Umar ؓ kissed the Black Stone, he said to it, "You don't give harm or benefit. If I didn't see the Prophet ﷺ kissing you, I would never kiss you."

Today people are dying to kiss the Black Stone. As reported by ibn 'Asaakir ؓ, Sayyidina 'Ali ؓ replied, "*Ya* 'Umar! Don't say that. That stone will witness for you on Judgment Day that you said *shahadah* there." And Sayyidina 'Umar ؓ said, "Sayyidina 'Āli ق saved twice in my life, and that was one of them."

Some people ask, "*Ya Rabbī*! We want to visit Your House, but we are unable. Are we going to be *mahrūmūn*, deprived of this *barakah*?" *Awliyaullah* say you can send *salam* from here, "*As-salam 'alayk, ya Ka'batullah! As-salam 'alayk, ya Baytullah Sharīf!*" *Allahu Akbar!* Do you think you cannot get that from here? Everything is determined according to our intention: to be there all the time, or to be in Allah's House all time, in Grandshaykh's presence all the time, or in the presence of Mawlana Shaykh Nazim al-Haqqani all the time! That will be accepted if we always seek that presence. Like how every day you want to see your children, your wife, mother, or brother, similarly you have to show your longing to be there.

That is why there are five prayers, as every prayer takes you there! Allah is the Most Merciful! Grandshaykh ق said, "If someone prays within one hour of the start of the prayer time, it is considered as if he went all the way to *Mecca al-Mukarramah*, stood facing *Ka'bah*, and prayed there. This *tajalli* was opened recently."

Awliyaullah inherit from the reality of *Ka'abatullah* so they can pass that to their followers. When they sit with their followers they pass heavenly lights, manifestations and energies, and the beauty and magnitude of such blessings cannot be described. Allah ﷻ describes Paradise as, "full of jewels, palaces, diamonds, food, silver pitchers, and young people serving you." Everything is described in a way so we might understand what is Paradise, but the real Paradise is to be in the Divine Presence, where *awliyaullah* are continuously trying to take their followers!

The benefits of the circle are for those in the circle, not those who are scattered about, and if the circle is tightly closed *Shaytan* cannot enter it. Did you see when they do *hadrah* in Cyprus, Mawlana Shaykh Nazim likes them to stay in circles? That is the right way; the Shaykh is in the circle and he sends the signals to those in the circle. We should not be arranged in rows like for prayers; *dhikrullah* always has to be in a circle. Without a circle, we are losing parts of these blessings. Instead of forming a human shield in the circle, *shayatīn* find gaps and enter.

The importance of *halaqah* is, the *Sahābah* ﷺ sat with the Prophet ﷺ in the *halaqah*, learning what they needed to know from him. He was the center of the circle, like *Ka'bah* is the center of earth where people focus their prayers. So in *dhikrullah*, when you are sitting in a circle you have to make sure that there is a center you focus on, just as when you pray you direct your face and your mind to *Ka'bah*, as it is the House of Allah. A reflection of the real *Ka'bah* is Bayt al-Ma'mūr in the Fourth Heaven, where Prophet ﷺ prayed with all Prophets in *Laylat al-Isrā' wal Mi'rāj*.

Imam Shafi'ī ق said the *halaqah* is a piece of Paradise where people sit and listen to or recite *dhikr*, and it cannot be other than that because of the *ahadīth* of the Prophet ﷺ:

When people sit remembering Allah, angels will encompass them.

There are angels roaming the streets looking for circles of dhikr to sit in, and Allah sent them there.

And he said angels in Heaven are continuously remembering in circles, so any circle people sit in remembering Allah ﷻ is in Paradise. Also, anyone who steps in Paradise cannot go to Hell. You are continuously entering a paradise when doing *dhikrullah*, so Allah ﷻ will take you to Paradise on your last breath.

ard al-halaqah ard al-jinān.

The earth of halaqah is the earth of Jannah.

Grandshaykh 'AbdAllah al-Fa'iz Daghestani ق wrote in his notes that Allah ﷻ will change that piece of land on which you sit and recite *dhikrullah* to a piece of Heaven, as angels cannot sit in a dirty place. We can sit in a place that is not clean because we are sinners, but angels cannot sit in a dirty place that stinks with our sins. Allah ﷻ promised His servants:

If you sit remembering Me, angels will come and Allah will remember you in a better place.

That means Allah ﷻ will change that place where you sit for *dhikr* to a heavenly place; otherwise angels cannot sit there. So for sure *halaqah adh-*

dhikr is important as it makes us enter Paradise, and when Allah gives something He will not take it.

That is why the Prophet ﷺ said, when you go to Madinatu 'l-Munawwarah:

> *Mā bayna qabrī wa minbarī rawdatan min riyādu'l-jannah.*
> *Between my grave and my pulpit is a garden from the gardens of Paradise."*
>
> (Ahmad)

Allah ﷻ made the *Rawdah* a piece of Heaven. That is why people wait hours to pray there, because when you put your feet in *Rawdah* between the *minbar* and Prophet's grave, you are entering Paradise and you will never see Hellfire! Similarly, anyone who enters a circle of *dhikr*, Allah ﷻ will dress them from those blessings and make his circle a circle in Paradise!

Here *awliyaullah* say something important: for a circle of *dhikr* to be considered a heavenly circle, it must meet nine conditions. Not any circle can be considered a circle of *dhikrullah,* although you might be doing *dhikr*. However, if that circle fulfilled the conditions, everyone sitting there doing *dhikrullah* will receive a reward more than that of fifty *shahīd*! Anyone who goes in that circle and observes all its conditions will have the reward of 70 or 100 *shahīd*, not 50. So if we are sitting in a circle remembering Allah ﷻ, saying, "*Lā ilāha illa-Llāh,*" with all its conditions then we will be rewarded more than 100 *shahīd* and that circle will be turned into a heavenly circle.

Conditions of a Heavenly Circle

First of its conditions is that there must be a head for *halaqah*, not one person leads one week and next week another person leads, but there must be an authorized one to lead that *halaqah*, with permission from his Shaykh and approved by all grandshaykhs, all the way to the Prophet ﷺ! Not just anyone may say, "I am leading the *halaqah*." He must have proper authority, otherwise the prerequisite of a heavenly *halaqah* is not met, and it will be only a normal *halaqah*.

Today so many people are trying to lead a *halaqah* of *dhikrullah* and there are differences between one *halaqah* and another; it depends where the authority is from (*idhn*).

Another condition is, all attendees must come only for the reason to attend *dhikrullah* and then depart with no discussion, no backbiting, no speaking, nothing. They come with full ablution, enter the *halaqah*, sit in their assigned places, do *dhikr* with the authorized Shaykh, and go home. There must be no speaking of anything related to *dunya*.

So what we are doing? It is not heavenly *halaqah* but rather a *halaqah* that takes away our sins. Allah has angels that will attend but they will not sit with us, they will be high above the circle. *Qasd al-jālisīn li julūsihim lil-'ibadat al-mutlaq*, only to sit and worship, nothing else, and everyone sitting in his assigned place. Like in a parking lot with assigned spaces, you must park only in your designated space, or in a conference you must sit in an assigned seat, nowhere else.

Here there is no discipline, so the benefit is not there, not as much as it should be.

Three Halaqahs of Shah Naqshband

Sayyidina Shah Naqshband had three weekly *halaqahs*. One was devoted to teaching *'ibadah, fiqh, hadīth* or *tafsīr al-Qur'an*, with no talk of *dunya*. If their homes were far, they brought their white clothes with them, went into a changing room, put on white robes and long dress, and then sat at their assigned seat. They knew who sat where, and who was to sit beside the Shaykh on his right and left, not like today with everyone pushing to sit next to the Shaykh. They had different levels to sit by the Shaykh's left or right; we don't see that. In previous times they came on time, and when the Shaykh arrived everyone was waiting in his seat on the floor. The Shaykh did not wait for people to arrive, and when he was ready to begin the door was locked and no one was allowed to enter. Students were required to wear white clothes and as the Shaykh spoke they wrote notes.

Another *halaqah* is devoted to *dhikrullah,* nothing else, in which all kinds of *'Asmaullah al-Husna* and different *sūrahs* were recited. They sat, recited, and departed the *halaqah* without any discussion or interaction.

The third type of *halaqah* included meditation, through which they connected their hearts with their Shaykh's heart. They sat on their knees with discipline for one or two hours. And all their focus is on love of Allah ﷻ, love of the Prophet ﷺ, and love of the Shaykh. Our *halaqah* is an imitation, like plastic fruit, but we are helpless and weak. We cannot be like them and we are asking Allah ﷻ to change our gathering from an imitational *halaqah* to a real *halaqah*.

In addition to wearing white clothes, sitting with discipline, and writing notes, the second condition is attendees must attend only for *'ibadah*, nothing else. Anything else makes the gathering like a soup of leftovers mixed with everything. Do you want delicacies or soup? Delicacies are expensive. If you want them, you need to sit in discipline and take from heavens; otherwise, everyone can take soup and drink it, no problem.

In that third type of *halaqah*, as soon as attendees sat they had no right to talk to each other, they only do their private *dhikr*, waiting for the Shaykh to arrive. As soon as the Shaykh sat in his place the *halaqah* was connected. All attendees were seated near each other, and when the Shaykh sat in his place the energy flowed from his right around the entire circle.

The third condition is, as soon as he sits, immediately he connects their hearts to the love of Allah ﷻ and to love of Prophet ﷺ. If they are disciplined and not coming except to do *dhikrullah*, he will cut their hearts from receiving any kind of gossips, *khawātir*, because he has that power. Good and bad gossips may come, but the Shaykh allows only the good inspirations in. He restricts the receiver of attendees; like parental controls on a cable TV box or on the Internet, he blocks unacceptable content. Through your own box everything comes: *Shaytan*, good inspirations, bad inspirations and gossips are all there. So *awliyaullah* put a parental lock and restrict bad content from entering attendees' hearts in that *halaqah*.

In this type of association, if they fulfilled the two conditions, then they are able to stop all gossips that come to the ears. Anything that is connected to *dunya* they put a lock on it and *Shaytan* cannot enter. However, at that time the *murīd* must accept what the Shaykh is trying to do; if he resists locking his box from gossips, the level of the association will go down because he contaminate others in the circle.

That is third condition and we leave the rest to next time, and there are nine of them.

So this is important, especially when you go to Cyprus, and attend *dhikr* in the *zawiya* of Mawlana. There is not like here. You have to be very careful as it is not like anywhere else, where people conduct *dhikr* with permission of Mawlana Shaykh. There must be more discipline and people must not gossip or make business there. Visitors come from far to visit, and must be disciplined to look only at their own conduct and not at what others are doing. For their visit to be accepted, visitors should remain secluded from *dunya* and do more *'ibadah*. As when you go for *Hajj*, the Prophet ﷺ said:

> *The one who doesn't make fitna or backbiting there will return pure like a newborn baby.*   Muslim

There are places around the world that inherit from that *hadith*, so those visiting *awliyaullah* will be granted many rewards and one of them is that they might be forgiven their sins, as Allah ﷻ said:

> *Behold! Verily on the friends of Allah there is no fear, nor shall they grieve; they who have attained to faith and have always been conscious of Him. For them there is the glad tiding (of happiness) in the life of this world and in the life to come; (and since) nothing could ever alter (the outcome of) God's promises, this is the triumph supreme!*   (Yūnus, 10:62-64)

Allah ﷻ will reward them and reward their students. So it is important when we visit Mawlana Shaykh in Cyprus to observe these conditions.

May Allah ﷻ forgive us and may Allah ﷻ bless us.

Wa min Allahi 't-tawfiq, bi hurmati 'l-habīb, bi hurmati 'l-Fatihah.

And with Allah is success. For the sake of the Beloved, for his sake we recite the opening chapter of Holy Qur'an.

꙰ 44 ꙰

The Power of Intercession

A'ūdhu billāhi min ash-Shaytani 'r-rajīm. Bismillāhi' r-Rahmāni 'r-Rahīm.
Nawaytu 'l-arbā'īn, nawaytu 'l-'itikāf, nawaytu'l-khalwah, nawaytu 'l-'uzlah,
nawaytu 'r-riyada, nawaytu 's-sulūk, lillāhi Ta'alā fī hādhā 'l-masjid.
Ati'ūllāha wa ati'ū 'r-Rasūla wa ūli 'l-amri minkum.
Obey Allah, obey the Prophet, and obey those in authority among you. (4:59)

On 2 *Sha'bān* 1330 *Hijra*, one-hundred years ago, this story was narrated by Sayyidina Shaykh Sharafuddin ق, our great-Grandshaykh. He said there was a deceased person and they wanted to pray on him and bury him. As soon as they put him in the coffin and began to carry him to the cemetery, they were unable. That was someone important in the community and a good person, so no one knew why one man, two men, three, five, fifty men, could not carry his coffin and it was stuck, glued to the earth.

Before we go in that story I want to narrate an event that happened with me and my brother in Tripoli, Lebanon, where there was a *wali* named Ahmad as-Sayyadi ق who was originally from Homs, Syria. Anyone could go to him, he had a house and a *maqām*, but he liked to stay in a shop in the downtown market, which was perhaps ten square feet. In winter he burned wood in a barrel to keep warm, and the shop was full of smoke. He sat doing *dhikr* and people came to him for advice. "This one is sick, this one died, this one needs this." He gave various *awrād* when they have difficulties. He was 115 years old when he died and we knew him fifteen years before he died.

Ahmad as-Sayyadi ق has a lot of followers. We lived in Tripoli, a big town in northern Lebanon with a population of at least two million. There they announced, "Shaykh Ahmad Sayyadi's home was hit by a rocket!" and everyone was concerned that he might die. We went to see him and *alhamdulillah*, he was okay. The rocket exploded inside the house and nothing happened to him, not one injury. Whom Allah ﷻ protects no one can injure, and Allah protects his *awliya*.

Miracles of Awliyaullah

Shaykh Ahmad as-Sayyadi ق had many miracles in Tripoli, where there are a lot of *awliya*. Mawlana Shaykh Nazim ق likes that city a lot. There is the

"Cemetery of *Awliya*" where only *awliya* are buried. The son of one *wali* told me, in WWII when the French Army was in the country, the government ordered from France a twenty-thousand ton cargo ship full of wheat for bread and cooking, and it also carryied food for the French army. There was war in the city and that ship approached the shore to empty its load. The authorities ordered the ship to move back out to sea, and that *wali*, whose name I cannot remember, sat fishing by the ocean. Suddenly people saw him cast his fishing line on the ship, as if he was fishing the ship. Residents pleaded with him to come inside as there was an intense bombardment.

He said, "No, I am not coming in."

He threw his fishing line and left it on the ship, and from the windows people said, "What are you doing?"

He said, "I am fishing the ship."

So when officials ordered the ship back out to sea, it did not move, although they used full engine power.

Then he said, "This ship is confiscated until all the food is distributed to the poor and not to the army." No one could move that Shaykh's hand. Hundreds of soldiers emptied the ship, then he moved his hand and the ship was able to leave the harbor!

Shaykh Ahmad as-Sayyadi ق died and his students decided to bury him in an area far outside the city. The *janaza* procession would have walked one hour from the *masjid* to the burial site, half-an-hour up a hill to a site where they wanted to build a huge *maqām*.

My brother and I told them, "It is better not to bury him there, but bury him in his own mosque, near the Cemetery of *Awliya*."

They said, "No way, no way!" They wanted to take him up that hill.

We said, "No, it is better to bury the *wali* where he wants to be buried. Use your minds."

They refused, so what to do; we had to go with them. One-hundred thousand people came for his *janaza* and they took him to the main mosque, the big mosque of Tripoli, which was quickly filled, so some prayed outside in the streets. Afterwards, the *janaza* procession moved along the route and when they arrived at that hill, it was not able to move; the coffin resisted. Ten, twenty, thirty men tried to move that coffin, and that *wali* did not weigh more than 100 lbs. as he was big worshipper and did not eat except three dates per day and some water, and yet no one could move his coffin further. They tried and the coffin pushed them back. They didn't know what to do.

We said, "Take him back. It might be he wants to go to his own place, in the Cemetery of *Awliya*."

They said, "No, it is impossible."

We said, "Try!"

As soon as they turned to go in that direction the coffin moved, but when they turned back towards the hill it stopped. So they decided to go back, and later they found in his will written instructions to bury him by his mosque and his street, so people can see him and he sees them and they recite *Fatihah* for him. That is to tell them, "I am nothing. You see me, I am by the street."

So *awliyaullah* have that kind of power; when they die they resist if they don't like something. Like today they don't let you open a grave. A government may want to open a highway and they want to take the shrine or grave of the *wali*, but they find resistance.

In Damascus, near the burial site of family members of the Prophet ﷺ, where Sayyidina Bilāl ؓ and many other *Sahābah* ؓ are also buried, there is a small cemetery where S'ād ad-Dīn Jibāwi ق, a Shaykh of *Ahlu 'l-Bayt* is buried. There, the government planned to build a highway, but on that site there was a mosque with a grave inside. How do you pray in a mosque with a grave? Allah ﷻ said in Surat al-Kahf, "Build a mosque on their graves," to make it a place where people can read *Fatihah* and do *dhikr*. So S'ād ad-Dīn Jibāwi's grave was there and they decided to relocate it. They brought a bulldozer and when it came to the wall of that *maqām* it shut down; the workers pushed it but it froze.

So they asked the Grand Mufti of Damascus what to do. He loved Grandshaykh 'AbdAllah ق and asked him, "What must we do?"

The Power of Dhikrullah

Grandshaykh ق said, "You cannot just take him. If you want to take him you have to make *dhikrullah* all night, then he will accept."

So they followed that advice and gathered many people and scholars, and went down to his grave and did *dhikr* all night long. Then the next day they brought the bulldozer and it was able to move, it took down the cemetery wall and then they came to the actual grave and when they opened it, a beautiful smell came out, and the grave was fresh, as if he was buried today. They built the new *masjid* by the side of the highway and put his grave there. *Awliya* have that power, both during their life and in their death, because Allah ﷻ gave them that freedom.

So in that story Great-Grandshaykh Sharafuddin ق mentioned a long time ago that no one can take that man out. Then they decided to bring more men but they could not take him up. Then one said, "The Shaykh is sending a message."

Shaykh Sharafuddin ق said, "If you want to take him, you have no choice but to do what Imam Shafi'i used to do."

Once in the time of Imam Shafi'i ؓ, a person died and no one knew who is that person. So according to Islamic *Shari'ah* they have to take care of him; they washed him and took his coffin, but they were not able to move it. So Imam Shafi'i ordered the people to sit in a circle and do *dhikrullah*; then they were able to take his coffin to the cemetery. Based on that, Shaykh Sharafuddin ق told them, "Do the same, then you will be able to take his body to the cemetery."

They called all *'ulama* and students, who sat in a circle and recited *dhikrullah* 70,000 times, sending the reward to that deceased person. As soon as they did that, the coffin moved and they felt it shaking. When they carried it, it was as light as a feather!

They asked, "What is the wisdom? Fifty people were not able to carry him before, and now with this recitation he can be carried?"

I am speaking on the importance of *halaqah* for *dhikrullah*, which cleans you of your sins. Wherever it is attend, and if not, do it by yourself. The only valid excuse not to attend is when you are sick or you are hosting an important guest or when you are traveling; then you are not obliged to go to the circle of *dhikrullah*. Other than that, in normal circumstances you must attend as there is lot of *barakah* in that for your life. That is why Grandshaykh ق never accepted anyone to miss *dhikrullah*; they must attend at least once a week.

The *dhikrullah* we are doing today, the small *khatm*, *Khatm as-Saghīr*, after Grandshaykh ق passed away usually Mawlana Shaykh did that in Western countries. There in Damascus he did the big *khatm* where we counted on pebbles. He advised the small *dhikr* to be done every day even, and the big one is done once a week. There is a lot of *barakah* in *dhikrullah* as it will clean all the sins and mistakes we have done from the past week to this week.

And they asked, "What was wrong with this person that we could not carry him from the floor?"

Shaykh Sharafuddin ق said, "That man was very pious, with very few sins; he didn't do anything wrong in his life. But his main problem was he had not taken care of his obligations. He does them, but carelessly. He doesn't commit sins but he doesn't take care of his religious obligations. He goes to his work, goes home, not backbiting or making *fitna*, but because he was careless, he fell into innovations."

When you are careless of your obligations, you begin to make *fatwa* to yourself and give excuses why not to take care of obligations. This creates innovation within you. We find now on the Internet "Grand Muftis"; they don't accept to be mufti only, they have to be Grand Mufti and they are bringing new stuff in Islam. *SubhanAllah*, this came now in Grandshaykh's notes, to tell those on the Internet and to say that too many of these so-called Shaykhs are falling and making their followers fall into innovations as they never studied *Shari'ah* and they were only given permission to lead *dhikr*. Instead, they began to give *irshād* (guidance) and made excuses on themselves, innovation, that their followers now also follow.

They will face a huge problem from that mistake. They mislead their followers from the right way, from *tarīqah*. *Tarīqah* is *azīmat ash-Shari'ah*, *tarīqah* is not *rukhsa*. The lowest level in *Shari'ah* is you give an excuse to yourself in every aspect of *Shari'ah*. "*Azīmah*" is not to accept any excuse in your obligation. So *tarīqah* is more stringent teachings of *awliya* and strict compliance with everything *Shari'ah* is asking. *Tarīqah* keeps the highest level of strictness and purity on yourself, to be good person with *adab* in all matters and performing all your obligations in the best possible way. That is why we say *tarīqah* is *azīmat ash-Shari'ah*, the highest level in which *Shari'ah* can be performed. That is why many people, with my respect to everyone, are falling into misleading ways, into deviation. They are praying but they innovate.

Kullu bida'tun dalāh wa kullu dalālatan fin-nār.
Every innovation is heresy and every heresy is in the Fire.

I am not citing this verse like some people who say it casually, without understanding. It is established in *tarīqah* that people must not go into *bidaʿ*, but ignorant, self-proclaimed Shaykhs mislead their students.

Wahabis accuse people of *bidaʿ* while they are the ones making *bidaʿ*! We in *tarīqah* say if you are not following *Shariʿah* you are making *bidaʿ*, your own way. But, it is correct that you cannot make your own way.

So the importance of *dhikrullah* is to clean. Shaykh Sharafuddin ق said, "This man was from pious people, he never did something wrong. He tried his best, although of course people make wrong, but he was not giving importance to his obligations, so many innovations came from him. When he was leaving *dunya* and Sayyidina Azraʿīl ؏, the Angel of Death, revealed to him all the innovations that he did in his life. When that opened to him, he felt he is from the People of Hellfire. He used to say like people today, "O nevermind, my Shaykh will defend me. O nevermind, this is *sunnah*, I don't need to do that."

You must have self-criticism. Mawlana Shaykh Nazim, may Allah give him long life, does not do any innovation, and I have been with him for fifty years. But some people around him do a lot of innovations. They don't know what they are doing, and I feel bad to mention what they are doing.

So when he felt he will be from the People of Hellfire, at that moment Prophet's ﷺ intercession came for him, because he was pious person. No, from whoever said, *Lā ilāha illa-Llāh* will enter Paradise. For sure, a Muslim doing *bidaʿ* will enter Paradise, from Allah's Mercy that He gave to Prophet ﷺ!

So as we said, when they put him in the coffin and began to recite, that coffin shook. He was feeling he was from the People of Hellfire so he resisted moving to his grave before the intercession of Prophet ﷺ came. He didn't have a Shaykh, so he was calling for intercession of Prophet ﷺ. The importance of having a Shaykh is to have one to defend you in that critical position. We ask Allah to keep us under mercy when he is taking back our souls and to keep us under protection and the intercession of Prophet ﷺ when we are in that position!

So when intercession of Prophet ﷺ came, he then felt free and the coffin began to move and shake. That intercession of Prophet ﷺ was due to the *dhikrullah* they had performed.

৪০ ... ০৪

I was going to mention about Somalia, where extremists have destroyed so many graves. Allah ﷻ doesn't like that. That is why punishment is coming on them. *Man adhā lī waliyyan adhantahu bi 'l-harb.* Allah ﷻ declared war on those who come against a *wali*. Allah will come against those who are destroying the graves of *awliyaullah*.

> *Fa qāl 'bnu 'alayhim bunyana. Rabbahum 'alāmū bihim.*
> They said, "Build on them a building that is a place of remembrance (that they are Ashāb al-Kahf)."   (Surat al-Kahf, 18:21)

That is why it is accepted in Islam to build a *masjid* over a grave. Let them read *Surat al-Kahf*. It means if a prophet goes away, build a building on them; he didn't say, "build on them *lawha* (panel, sign)." *Bunyana* means "building." The others said, "Build a *masjid* over them." So you have two choices. How do you say no? This is sign of Islam. The Turkish built *masajid* all around Europe. Even in Andalusia, everyone knows Islam was there, all these different writings and even graves of *Sahābah* ؓ are there, some well-known and some unknown died there. *Fatihah.*

Insha'Allah we can continue to broadcast from Cyprus, although there are many problems there, both physical and political. Some people tried to stop it and others tried to keep it, and we are in a struggle. May Allah make it easy. Mawlana Shaykh Nazim ق is happy to address and reach everyone; that is most important. Of course he can reach people by spirituality and we understand that, but people like to see him in his house. Some said, "We don't want any broadcast from here." Some think they are the bosses. They said, "We don't want anyone to come to Mawlana. We can record him and you can put it on your website in the evening." That is what they tried to do, but *makarū wa makarullah*, "Allah planned and destroyed their plan," as they are *Shaytan*'s plans. They poisoned Prophet ﷺ and cast evil spells on him! So don't say in Mawlana's house there is no *Shaytan*; there are many, even some in human shape, and there are a lot of *munāfiqūn*!

> *Yaqūlūna bi'afwhihim mā laysa fi qulūbihim.*
> "... saying with their mouths what is not in their hearts."
>   (Surat Āli-'Imrān, 3:167)

May Allah ﷻ forgive us and may Allah ﷻ bless us.

Wa min Allahi 't-tawfīq, bi hurmati 'l-habīb, bi hurmati 'l-Fatihah.
And with Allah is success. For the sake of the Beloved, for his sake we recite the opening chapter of Holy Qur'an.

There Is No Rest in Religion

*A'ūdhu billāhi min ash-Shaytani 'r-rajīm. Bismillāhi' r-Raḥmāni 'r-Raḥīm.
Nawaytu 'l-arbā'īn, nawaytu 'l-'itikāf, nawaytu'l-khalwah, nawaytu 'l-'uzlah,
nawaytu 'r-riyaḍa, nawaytu 's-sulūk, lillāhi Ta'alā fī hādhā 'l-masjid.
Ati'ūllāha wa ati'ū 'r-Rasūla wa ūli 'l-amri minkum.
Obey Allah, obey the Prophet, and obey those in authority among you. (4:59)*

Two words which are light on the tongue and heavy on the Scales on Judgment Day: *SubhanAllah wa bi-hamdihi, SubhanAllahi 'l-'Azhīm*, Glory be to Allah, Glory be to Allah, the Tremendous!

No one suffered what Sayyidina Muhammad ﷺ suffered, abuse from his own tribe, his own people and from the unbelievers. They tortured him and abused him! On the other side, we cannot say he suffered, but we can say he is the Perfect Man that Allah created, the Perfect Human Being. He also didn't rest any moment in his life without continuous worshipness day and night, and he said, "*lā rāhata fī 'd-dīn*, There is no rest in religion."

How can you rest? If someone told you, "I will give you this small island worth millions as a resort, but you have to do your best for me and work for me all your life and I will give you that," you would work without saying you are tired! Everyone looks out for their own benefit. There is no doubt you will work hard to get what you want.

So besides being tortured by unbelievers and idol-worshippers, Sayyidina Muhammad ﷺ dedicated his life to his Lord. Sayyida A'yesha said that from standing day and night in prayer his feet were swollen, and she asked him, "O Prophet of Allah! For sure Allah has forgiven whatever you have done of sins past or future." The Prophet replied, "O A'yesha, shall I not be a thankful servant?" The feet of inheritors of Prophet ﷺ get swollen in their worship day and night; that reflects on them from the Prophet. Look at Mawlana Shaykh Nazim and see.

So you try your best and dedicate your life struggling for *dunya* and *Ākhirah*. *Ya Rabbī, Anta Maqsūdī*, "O my Lord, You are my aim!" It means, "I don't want *dunya* or *Ākhirah*; You are my aim and I want You to be satisfied with me!" That is what Prophet ﷺ said. So for sure those who have the physical blood of the Prophet or who have the spiritual light in them will face problems, but what you face compared to what the Prophet ﷺ faced is a drop in an ocean!

Alhamdulillah, you encountered a problem that you are struggling against and at least it didn't go further than that. If two people are fighting, it is best to split them up because if they keep fighting one might kill the other. Relax and submit to Allah ﷻ.

The problem is we cannot submit because we say it is humiliating. If you say, "I forgive him (or her)" you think you will humiliate yourself, but if you don't humble yourself you will never reach the Divine Presence. When you act humbly, Allah ﷻ sends rewards and more blessings.

Whoever forgives and makes peace gets reward from Allah.

(Surat ash-Shura, 42:40)

How to Enter Maqam al-Ihsan

You don't want to get revenge with your hand directly. Forgive and Allah ﷻ gives more. Struggling is very difficult for us. That anger within us makes us rebel and will never let us overcome our ego. So what extra worship do *awliyaullah* perform? They pray, you pray; they fast, you fast; they make *dhikr*, you make *dhikr*. Whatever you make extra they make the same as they are giving you what to do. But they went into seclusion to purify from the sediment of the self; they purify themselves of bad characteristics. So that is why they enter *Maqām al-Ihsan*, "the Station of Perfected Character." So as soon as you throw out bad characteristics, you enter the first step in *Maqām al-Ihsan* and they begin to remove the veils.

The problem is that we don't do what they tell us! We don't want to make progress, but they want to face a lot of obstacles in purifying themselves. You fast, they fast. You eat, they eat. They like to joke, no problem. You marry, they marry. You have children, they have children. You pray at night, they pray at night. So what more do they do? They entered the *Maqām al-Ihsan*. They do voluntary worship and we don't, and that is the problem.

What is voluntary worship? They feel with people, they share what they have with people, they give advice to help people, they overcome their ego. Our ego rides us, but they ride their ego and make it under them. *Nafsuka mati'atuka*, "Your self is your ride," not, "you are the ride of the self." You make your self the horse. Now *Shaytan* and ego ride us! That is the big difference. When they throw all these bad characteristics, Allah ﷻ

opens for them the state of love mentioned in a very authentic *hadīth* that is like revelation, the *Hadīth Qudsī*.

> *As much as My servant approaches Me through voluntary worship, I love him. When I love him, I will be his eyes that he can see with, his ears that he can hear with, his tongue that he can speak with, his hand that he can touch with, and his feet that he can walk with.* (Bukhari)

Allah will give through love. Do we have love to Allah? No, we have love of *dunya*. We run after *dunya* and *awliya* run after Allah. These are differences in behavior and taste. The others are obligations. When you enter diplomatic status they teach you etiquettes: how to laugh, walk, talk and smile. True diplomats never have bad manners. In politics, they never teach you to hurt anyone's feelings, but we hurt each other's feelings. May Allah forgive us and protect us for the sake of Prophet, for the sake of *awliyaullah,* for the sake of *Ramadan*.

Afa 'an man asa ilayk, "Forgive the one who harmed you." It means anyone who harmed your reputation, or by what he did or was supposed to do and didn't, forgive them; no need to complain. If something happened it will pass, you will move forward, and Allah will give you better. May Allah forgive us.

During hunger, be patient one hour or a half-hour and then you are no longer hungry. It is ego that makes you feel hungry. I know people who live all their lives on water only, no food. *Awliyaullah* are always in seclusion!

May Allah forgive us and may Allah bless us.

Wa min Allahi 't-tawfiq, bi hurmati 'l-habīb, bi hurmati 'l-Fatihah.
And with Allah is success. For the sake of the Beloved, for his sake we recite the opening chapter of Holy Qur'an.

Stories of Awliya and Their Murids: 'Ubaydullah al-Amawi

A'ūdhu billāhi min ash-Shaytani 'r-rajīm. Bismillāhi' r-Rahmāni 'r-Rahīm.
Nawaytu 'l-arbā'īn, nawaytu 'l-'itikāf, nawaytu'l-khalwah, nawaytu 'l-'uzlah,
nawaytu 'r-riyāda, nawaytu 's-sulūk, lillāhi Ta'alā fī hādhā 'l-masjid.
Ati'ūllāha wa ati'ū 'r-Rasūla wa ūli 'l-amri minkum.
Obey Allah, obey the Prophet, and obey those in authority among you. (4:59)

From where to begin, where to end? *Mā'rīfatullah*[4] is so huge that it is very difficult to understand, except when you are in the presence of a *sultān*, a *wali*. We spoke of 'Abdur-Rahīm al-Māghribi ق, and how much he tried in the presence of Sayyidina 'Abdul-Khāliq al-Ghujdawāni ق, but with all his questions how he failed without submission. *Awliyaullah* have stories about their followers so others will learn. Without stories human beings cannot understand. Allah gave human beings the ability to like all kinds of stories. So if you want to give them knowledge, phrase it in a way that includes a story, and they will understand.

The human mind is limited, and these stories about *murīd*s and their Shaykh are the lowest examples of knowledge, because the *wali* goes down all the way to the level of the student. So stories of *awliyaullah* with their students are like cartoons, and that attracts people and they will be interested. If there is no story, they have no interest. If you speak day and night about *'azhamatullah*, Allah's Greatness, it doesn't stay in their mind. But if you narrate a story, they retain that knowledge, as evidenced in Holy Qur'an:

Nahnu naqussu 'alayka ahsana al-qasasi bimā awhayna ilayka hadha 'l-Qur'ana wa in kunta min qablihi la-mina 'l-ghafilīn.

We do relate to you the most beautiful of stories, in that We reveal to you this (portion of the) Qur'an: before this, you were also among those who knew it not. (Surat Yūsuf, 12:3)

"We narrate to you the best of stories in which We have revealed to you the Holy Qur'an, *Ya Muhammad*." Allah ﷻ only likes the best. That is

---

[4] Knowledge of Allah ﷻ.

why Allah doesn't look at dirtiness of human beings. His mercy is so huge that He doesn't look at anything bad His servants do, He looks only at their good deeds.

So the Holy Qur'an is full of stories, to teach us. We begin our discussion today with a story according to Grandshaykh's ق notes, of Sayyidina 'Abdul-Khāliq al-Ghujdawāni ق with one of the *'ulama*, 'Ubaydullah al-Amawi ق, dated 21 Muharram 510 A.H.

The Evolution of Naqshbandi Tariqah

Sayyidina 'Abdul-Khāliq al-Ghujdawāni ق sat with his followers for *Khatm al-Khawajagan*. He is the head, the *khalīfatullah* of the *khatm*. The origin of the *khatm* came, as *awliyaullah* mention, when the Prophet was migrating from Mecca to Madinah with his *sāhib* (companion) in the cave Ghari Thawr, hiding from the unbelievers who intended to kill him. One of the wisdoms, a secret of that cave, is in the beginning of *Khatm al-Khawajagan*, *dhikrullah* upon which Sayyidina 'Abdul-Khāliq al-Ghujdawāni ق received his *khulafat* from the Prophet ﷺ and from Allah ﷻ to conduct *Khatm al-Khawajagan*.

In that cave, when Prophet ﷺ stopped the snake from eating the leg of Sayyidina Abu Bakr as-Siddiq ق, Allah ﷻ ordered him to order all Prophets, all *awliya*, and all *Naqshbandiyya* (souls) to appear. In the time of the *Sahābah* ؓ, what we know today as "*Naqshbandiyya*" was called "*Siddiqiyya*." In time of Sayyidina Bayazid, our *tarīqah* was called "*Tayfuriyya*." Then when it spread throughout the Far East and Far West by Shah Naqshband, it was called "*Naqshbandiyya*." Today it is called "*Haqqani*" as it spread further east and west by Mawlana Shaykh Nazim al-Haqqani ق. It is also called "*Mujadiyya*" and in Southeast Asia you find a lot of the "*Khalidiyya*" branch, as it was spread by Sayyidina Khalid al-Baghdadi ق. And so in every century it was called something based on the current Shaykh of *tarīqah*.

So in that cave, Prophet ﷺ ordered Sayyidina 'Abdul-Khāliq al-Ghujdawāni ق to be the leader of this original secret of that Way to continue up to Judgment Day. He ordered all Naqshbandi souls to appear and Sayyidina 'Abdul-Khāliq al-Ghujdawāni ق led the *dhikr* there. Anyone who appeared in that cave will appear in *dunya*. Even if he came only once to a *Naqshbandiyya Khatm al-Khawajagan*, it means he is part of that appearance in the Ghari Thawr. Once a person sits in our *khatm*, it means he is related to Shah Naqshband, all the way back to Sayyidina Abu Bakr as-Siddiq ق and the Prophet ﷺ in that cave, and that person is under the guidance of a *wali*.

This is not restricted to the Haqqani branch, but applies to all branches of Naqshbandiyya.

Grandshaykh ق says recitation will put them inside that cave. There are thousands of branches, but where is the secret, that is something else. Anyone who says he is following the Naqshbandi Tarīqah, whoever his Shaykh is, his soul must have been present in Ghari Thawr. And the *khalīfatullah*, the leader for that *khatm* is Sayyidina 'Abdul-Khāliq al-Ghujdawāni ق; Allah gave him that specialty.

He knows by name all souls who were present in Ghari Thawr, what they are doing in their life, what will happen to them, and every small detail about them from the Day of Promises until they go to Paradise on the Day of Judgment. He knows how long they are going to live and how many breaths they are going to breathe. When that *murīd* is about to die, Sayyidina 'Abdul-Khāliq ق appears, as *awliya* are free to move, and he makes them recite *talqīn adh-dhikr*.[5] He puts on their tongue the secret of the *dhikr* in that cave.

Don't think his movement takes time; he has the ability to shrink time and space, by Allah's Order, just as Allah ﷻ ordered him, "Ya 'Abdul-Khāliq! Take your stick and go to Merv (his village) to that huge rock and hit your stick on it." When he hit that rock, it cracked and water gushed out; to this day people drink from that water. Allah ﷻ said, "Ya 'Abdul-Khāliq al-Ghujdawāni ق! Your responsibility from now to the Day of Judgment is that I am going to create from every drop of water an angel and whom you must name, and every name must be unique; you cannot give two angels the same name."

In *dunya*, can anyone find a unique name that no other person has? Imagine naming the countless drops in a waterfall, each with a unique name unlike no other. And Allah ﷻ said all these angels created up to Judgment Day will be divided and assigned to different people, and their praises will be written on that person's account.

Let us call it *Siddiqiyya*, as *Naqshbandiyya* comes from two different sources: Sayyidina Abu Bakr as-Siddiq ق and Sayyidina 'Āli ق. They come together in Sayyidina Ja'far as-Sādiq ق. So in reality Sayyidina Ja'far is "of the two wings," as he combined the two streams of knowledge, Abu Bakr

---

[5] *Talqīn*, "to put on the tongue."

as-Siddiq, Salman al-Farsi, Qassim, and Sayyidina Ja'far is fourth in the *silsilah*, may Allah preserve their secrets. Then he gave to Sayyidina Bayazid al-Bistāmi and 'Ubaydullah al-Amawi ق. He is from Shām (Damascus); then Shām and Baghdad were fountains of knowledge.

They don't call themselves "'*abdAllāh*," because they don't consider they deserve that title; instead they call themselves "'*ubayd*." Do you know the difference between '*abd* and '*ubayd*? "'*Abd*" is "servant" and "'*ubayd*" is "servant of the servant of the servant of the servant; the lowest of servants." Now we say "'Abdul-Hamid," "'Abdul-Hafiz," but when people say the names, they leave off "'*abd*" and say only the name, which is *haram*, as these are Allah's Beautiful Names and Attributes.

So he said, "Tell me what is in your heart."

The Central Role of Obedience in Spiritual Development

In this story we examine the importance of the sight of the master, and how much he will pour into your heart when you are submitting. When you are not submitting, you are still like children like kindergarten. The more you shout at them the more they rebel. The rebellious nature is in all of us, as we are all raised as children. That nature prevents you from accepting any order as you want to do what you want to do. That is why in the army they teach you discipline. If you don't like the order given to you by the commander, still you must execute it. Then you can go to your room and shout until you explode, but you must listen and obey.

Sami'na wa ata'na ghufranak rabbana wa ilayk al-masīr.

We hear and we obey, your forgiveness we seek O our Lord, and to You is the journey.

After obedience comes forgiveness. When you listen and obey Allah, then forgiveness comes. When you listen and obey the Prophet ﷺ then forgiveness comes, as Allah ﷻ said:

Man 'ata ar-rasul faqad ata'Allah.

Who obeys the Prophet in fact obeys Allah.

When you obey your teacher, then *mā'rifat* will come and heavenly knowledge will be poured in your heart. So come with submission, not with questions; don't come with questions, like 'Abdur-Rahīm al-Māghribi ق did. He came as if to tell Shaykh 'Abdul-Khāliq al-Ghujdawāni ق, "I know about this level of *wali* and this level and this level and this level: four levels of knowledge." And Shaykh 'Abdul-Khāliq al-Ghujdawānī ق said no for each one, meaning, "Don't come to me and teach me with your knowledge. Submit!"

So 'Ubaydullah al-Amawi ق came with submission. When Shaykh 'Abdul-Khāliq al-Ghujdawānī ق sat with his students, all of them gave their hearts to the Shaykh, all sat with discipline in his assigned place; you cannot sit in the place of someone else and they knew where to sit, without it being written. Might be you sit twenty or even thirty years and someone comes in one day and he gets what the one who came for thirty years did not yet receive. Now this one never came to Shaykh 'Abdul-Khāliq al-Ghujdawānī ق and now on the date 21 Muharram 510 Hijri, he came. As soon as he entered, usually they go to their place and sit, they don't talk. This one foreigner entered and sat at the end, and Shaykh 'Abdul-Khāliq al-Ghujdawānī ق said, "Come sit in the middle," because he believed he is weak and helpless. Don't object in your heart, because our heart is always criticizing. (Mawlana teases one murid.) You are sleepy a little bit. So now your heart is saying to you, "Sleep, sleep, sleep!" It is better, *nawm azh-zhalim 'ibadah*, "Sleep of an oppressor is worship."

So don't criticize and complain if the Shaykh calls a new one, "Come sit with me." Don't say, "O, I am with Shaykh for thirty years and I can't sit near him." You don't know the hearts, they know the hearts.

So that Shaykh, 'Ubaydullah al-Amawi ق, was called to sit in the middle and Shaykh 'Abdul-Khāliq al-Ghujdawānī ق said, "*Ya* 'Ubaydullah! Tell me what kind of inspiration came to your heart now?" He wants to teach everyone. With one person he can teach everyone, and he wants that person to say in public, that with twenty-five years of sitting with *awliyaullah,* still he is in need of the Shaykh's vision, or sight, as we said.

'Ubaydullah al-Amawi ق said, "*Ya Sayyidi*! For twenty-five years I am struggling, making all kinds of efforts from a weak, helpless servant to reach my aim, *mā'rīfatullah*, to know my Lord."

Sayyidina Ahmad al-Badawi didn't say, "O my Lord, give me *mā'rīfatullah*!" He said, "O my Lord! Open your Divine Presence for me!" Look how the ego differs from one to another. Allah ﷻ sent someone to him, who said, "Do you want the key, O Ahmad?" and he answered, "No, I want the key from the Keymaker." He was asking for the Divine Presence, like those today who want to go directly. Can you go visit a president of a country directly? So he left him to wander for six months with no key.

'Ubaydullah al-Amawi ق answered, "For twenty-five years I have been a weak servant coming to your door, struggling to reach something. I am not saying I want to reach everything. Now I came to your association thinking to myself, wondering with astonishment, can I receive from Shaykh 'Abdul-Khāliq al-Ghujdawāni ق something that takes me to my goal? *Ilahī Anta maqsūdī wa ridāka matlūbī!*[6] So *Sayyidi*, I was hoping my aim will be fulfilled when I sat in this association and you were conducting the *dhikr*. Can I reach that?"

The Wrestler Who Submitted

One wrestler came to Great-Grandshaykh Sharafuddin ق seeking *tarīqah*, saying, "Shaykh!" He had no respect for the Shaykh. It means, "This is only between you, the Shaykh, and me, the wrestler!"

Boxers are ego fighters, like two roosters in a cockfight. In many countries, they put black magic on both roosters and they fight, one to kill the other. That is why when you are affected by black magic you have to slaughter a rooster and drop that blood on the ground, and *insha'Allah*, Allah ﷻ will cure you of black magic.

He was not asking for the ego. If he was asking for ego, Allah will tell him, "I will not open the door for you."

So he said, "Can I receive *ma'rifatullah* in this association?" and the Shaykh was looking and seeing his heart and seeing it clean, just like the wrestler coming to Great-Grandshaykh ق with his hat cocked sideways, carrying a knife, a gun, and a dagger, and his hat was cocked sideways on his head! He said, "Shaykh! I want *tarīqah*! If you don't give *tarīqah*..." He had a machine gun. So the Shaykh looked at his heart and found it clean. And you know the story, but we will summarize it.

So the Shaykh said, "You want *tarīqah*? Okay, stay here tonight," as he was in seclusion in the mountains. "Tomorrow morning we will see."

So he was happy, he slept, rested, and came to the Shaykh the next morning, saying, "Shaykh! I want *tarīqah*!"

---

[6] "(O Allah!) You are my goal and I want You to be happy and satisfied with me."

What *tarīqah*? All *tarīqah* is based on one thing, not on knowledge. You have to do obligations, prayers and fasting. But that is not the basis to receive spiritual dress by reading or through books; it is something within you that you must clean. It is within you; you have to throw it out of yourself. If you are angry you cannot receive *tarīqah*, and that means angry about anything. You have to be calm, patient. If your wife shouts at you, open one ear, close one ear. If you shout at your wife, she has to open both ears and close both ears! You are not hearing, so why have a problem about it?

So the Shaykh said, "Tomorrow, go downtown and you will find a butcher carrying on meat his shoulders. Go from behind him and slap him on his neck with all your power, then return to me."

That wrestler thought, *"Masha'Allah, tarīqah* is very nice, slapping people! I want spend a long time this *tarīqah."* So he went, found that person and slapped him. That person looked at him with anger, but continued on his way. The wrestler wanted to fight, but that person didn't respond. So the next day, so he came and told the Shaykh, who said, "Okay, tomorrow go find someone carrying intestines and stomachs of sheep, and slap him with all your might." The next day the wrestler found that one and slapped him, causing the intestines and stomachs to fall on that one's head. The wrestler became angry because this one didn't show any anger; he laughed!

On the third day, the wrestler told the Shaykh what happened and the Shaykh said, "Go find an old man plowing his field and beat him until your stick breaks on his back!" The wrestler did that and, to his astonishment, the old man said, "Forgive me! Don't come against me on the Day of Judgment as I injured your hand when you beat me!"

The wrestler returned to the Shaykh, who explained, "Okay, the first one is new in *tarīqah* and still has ego. The second one did not show anger but laughed, which means he is saying, 'I know you, my Shaykh, sent him to me.' But the third had no anger; truly, he has achieved submission."

Anger is the problem. Until you rid your heart of anger you remain in the same place, never making progress or achieving anything meaningful. In a tornado, the worst damage results from the eye. The anger of nature is concentrated in the center, and the outward part of the tornado produces less damage. That is the movement of *jinn*.

Shaykh 'Abdul-Khāliq al-Ghujdawānī ق said to him, *"Ya waladī*. Allah sent you here to fulfill your aim. It is written on the Day of Promises when I observed the Preserved Tablet that you will come at a precise moment, and that day I was waiting for you."

Shaykh 'Abdul-Khāliq ق revealed it to him, not like the first one ('Abdur-Rahīm al-Māghribi ق) who asked so many questions! He continued, "*Ya waladī*, first you need to throw anger from your heart, and you achieved that."

For twenty-five years, that scholar threw anger from his heart, following the *hadīth* of Prophet ﷺ:

Man 'arafa nafsahu faqad 'arafa rabbahu.
Who knows his self knows his Lord.

He went from one teacher to another to understand his self. Today no one wants to learn that, they only want to learn about faults of their partner, to whom they cannot yield, saying, "He/she does not understand me!" If first you understand your 'self,' you will understand the whole community.

It is difficult, as you have to obtain one key. If you miss one digit on an ATM code, you cannot access your bank account. In *tarīqah*, if you miss your key you cannot access your self. That is the meaning of, "Who knows his self knows his Lord." The one who opens all the digits of his password is able to access his self. Like computer hackers who extract locked data, there are also spiritual hackers. You have to be very experienced to get the password and hack the heart! *Awliya* say, "You don't have to go so far; we will give it to you quickly if you throw anger from your heart."

Look at the example of the old man whom the wrestler beat so harshly. Use earplugs to block external influence and don't listen to gossip, as even one word can provoke your anger.

Sayyidina 'Abdul-Khāliq al-Ghujdawāni ق said, "'Ubaydullah, you took away anger. I can give you your trust now. Be relaxed. You came to the source and I will fill you with all kinds of *altāf*, subtleties, and all good characteristics, gifts, and rewards that could be given to a servant of Allah! I can tell you the moment when your heart began to receive those rewards since twenty-five years ago, when you began to ask for it. They poured it in your heart, but some digits are missing there. I will show you how to enter into *mā'rifatullah*, knowledge of Allah ﷻ."

SubhanAllah! How much power these *awliya* have and how weak we are!

When the Shaykh Opens Your Trust

Sayyidina 'Abdul-Khāliq al-Ghujdawānī ق opened six powers to his heart, and he recited:

> He sends down water from the skies, and the channels flow, each according to its measure, but the torrent bears foam that mounts up to the surface. Even so, from that (ore) which they heat in the fire to make ornaments or utensils with, there is a scum. Thus does Allah (by parables) show forth truth and vanity, as the scum disappears like froth cast out while that which is for the good of mankind remains on the earth. Thus does Allah set forth parables.
>
> (Surat ar-Ra'd, 13:17)

'Ubaydullah al-Amawi ق didn't understand why Sayyidina 'Abdul-Khāliq ق read that *ayah* at that moment. The Shaykh said to him, "Ya 'Ubaydullah! This *ayah* I am reciting is for you only, not for others sitting in that circle. This *ayah* is your *hidayah*, guidance, and its secrets will only reach you."

Allah ﷻ put specific guidance in an *ayah* for each individual creature of His creation as their exclusive code. The Shaykh is saying, "Your guidance is within the secret of that *ayah*. I looked at your destiny on the Day of Promises, on the Preserved Tablet, and I know what to recite specifically for you, so that you receive your code."

All of them have to coincide with each other. That tunnel that you have to go through to reach your trust is the tunnel of that *ayah*. If you completed *'ibadat al-thaqalayn*, the worship of *jinn* and *ins* (humans), from the beginning of life to the end of life in full worshipness, still you will never reach *mā'rīfatullah* or your secrets from your own actions. You cannot reach your destiny or aim of *mā'rīfatullah* if you cannot understand the verse.

Allah said, "Enter homes through their doors," and your door is that *ayah*! Even if you pray day and night, without that *ayah* you will never reach your aim, *mā'rīfatullah*. The Shaykh is saying, "If I looked at you day and night without that *ayah* that has your secrets embedded in it, I will never be able to get you to the goal of reaching real realities; no one will be able to get you there without that *ayah*."

That is why it is said, "The ways to Allah ﷻ are on the number of breaths of humans." There is a way for every human based on an *ayah*. It is the responsibility of the highest caliber *wali* to look at his followers and know which *ayah* is for them. Each one has a different *ayah* of Qur'an and that is why *shuyukh* take one verse from here, one from here, one from here, and them put together and give to their *murīds* to read.

Like what we recite in morning, *shahidAllahu annahu lā ilāha illa Hū*, etc., are combined from different *ayah*. Also, the preparation for secrets to be opened to you is combined from different *ayah* of Qur'an, or else the combination won't open the lock. So everyone has a different lock with a different combination and different realities.

Salat-an-Najāt has a special combination of *ayah* that everyone reads the same, but that is a special combination for that prayer. But for individual *murīds* there are special *ayah* and when you say, "O my Shaykh! Look at me!" he has to look at you with the specific verse that relates to you. If he doesn't look at you with that, that light will not reach you; it is there but will not be open to you. Everyone has a *manba'*, a source of guidance, a spring that is exclusive to him or her. Don't say, "Why his source is that?" Each person has a different spring.

People are of two types. One type reaches Allah ﷻ through causes: if they do this, they get that, *bi'l-asbāb*. They have to keep running and doing, and from that they move forward through *kasban*, earning it. The other type is *wahban*, who reach Allah ﷻ through a grant. They may have a foul tongue and do not respect others, but you see them reaching higher spiritual states. Allah grants to them, so no one can question why they are making progress.

The twelve sons of Sayyidina Yaqub are Prophets, and Sayyidina Yusuf is a prophet and messenger. Those who threw Sayyidina Yusuf in the well were granted prophecy. Can anyone question why? Allah granted it to them.

Awliyaullah know which type of person you are. You receive through *wahban* (grant) or *kasban* (earning). Accordingly, there is a verse in Holy Qur'an that relates to specifically to you, to open in your heart different *haqa'iq*, realities. When Sayyidina 'Abdul-Khāliq ق read that *ayah*, it opened realities to 'Ubaydullah al-Amawi ق's heart.

When you need to purify yourself, you make ablution and the water cleans you. Without ablution you cannot pray, and if you did more than that and need a shower, you cannot take ablution and pray, you must take a *ghusl* (prescribed shower), or else you will remain in the pleasure of *dunya* and the shower takes you from *dunya* to *Ākhirah*.

Hadath al-Akbar, the greater impurity, requires a shower. If you touch your wife (intimately) it takes sins away, and if she touches you it takes sins away, but afterwards you must take a shower as it will purify you, as Allah ﷻ said:

We made from water every living thing. Will they not then believe?
(Surat al-Anbiya, 21:30)

Your body and your spirit become alive after you take a shower. Do ablution and you enter your prayer as if you are newly born. Also you sit in association and make *dhikr*, the heavenly manifestation of Allah's Beautiful Names and Attributes will shower you and purify you as if newly born. That is why it is important to attend *halaqat adh-dhikr* as it is cleansing process. Without a valid excuse to not attend, you miss one of the main pillars of *tarīqah*. Like we have five pillars of *Shari'ah* that you must fulfill, there are also pillars in *tarīqah*. Absence from *dhikrullah* is allowed on three occasions: when traveling, when hosting an important guest, or when you are very ill[7]; otherwise, you must attend.

Today all of us feel very heavy when it is time for *dhikrullah* and we try to postpone it as much as we can, even fifteen minutes. That association will shower and clean you, because that *barakah* will continue to run in that place until Judgment Day, and if you enter that place anytime in the week, that *tajalli* is still there.

That is why where any *wali* enters, his *tajalli* never leaves that place, which becomes a *maqām*, spiritual station. So make sure your Shaykh will sleep in your bed five minutes at least and that will become a *maqām*! Grandshaykh ق and Mawlana Shaykh are opening that secret and now I understand, when he visits someone's home and asks to rest, that is to make that reality stay there and it becomes a blessed house.

---

[7] Here "illness" connotes being so incapacitated that you would not go even if paid two gold coins.

That is why Sayyida Maryam's place is holy. Although Sayyidina Zakariyya ؑ is a prophet and higher, he needed to go to her room to supplicate:

Hunālika daʿā zakarīya rabbahu qāla rabbi hab lī min ladunka dhurrīyatan Tayyibatan 'innaka samīʿu ad-duʿā.

At that time Zakariyya invoked his Lord, saying, "O my Lord! Grant me from You a good offspring. You are indeed the All-Hearer of invocation."

(Surat Āli-'Imrān, 3:38)

And that is where he prayed and Allah ﷻ granted him a child, Sayyidina Yahya ؑ, which means "from life." That is *hayyat* (life) that Allah ﷻ gave to Sayyidina Zakariya's wife, Sarah.

That became a holy place where *duʿa* is accepted because of the *barakah* of that *dhikr*. That *barakah* always remains. So when Sayyidina 'Abdul-Khāliq al-Ghujdawāni ق read that verse of Holy Qur'an, from that verse he pulled all those embedded blessings, lights, and heavenly water that makes everything alive, and dressed 'Ubaydullah al-Amawi ق with that. At that moment, Sayyidina 'Ubaydullah became light and entered spiritual flight. He received not all, but quite a bit of his secrets, and that *ayah* became his daily *wird*.

That is why sometimes *awliya* tell you to recite a specific *ayah* and you don't know why. That means you must recite it without abandoning it. Once Mawlana Shaykh suddenly told me, "Read that *ayah* seven times daily." I was surprised. Then the next day he said, "If anyone is sick, read that *ayah* on them." There are 12,000 oceans of knowledge on every letter of Holy Qur'an, so how many secrets are on every *ayah*? Each recitation is different; today's recitation is different from yesterday's or tomorrow's. If a *wali* is unable to assign that *ayah*, he cannot take his *murīd* to the place he is aiming for.

People might ask, "Why don't we get our *ayah*?" Because we are donkeys and are not trying to submit. As long as we are not submitting, if one atom of pride or arrogance or anger remains, they will not give it! You have to completely submit to your Shaykh, who, from that recitation, will then take you to two spiritual levels, the first being Maqām at-Tawhīd, because he is big scholar.

Today big scholars say you have to be *muwahid*, one who does make *shirk* (associate partners with Allah); you have to submit to Allah's Oneness and say, *"Lā ilāha illa-Llāh"* or they don't consider you a real *muwahid*. Then after making all these stipulations, they say now you are eligible to say, *"Lā ilāha illa-Llāh"* and it is accepted.

However, after all these six powers opened to Sayyidina 'Ubaydullah ؓ, still he hadn't reached Maqām at-Tawhīd. In reality, if you say, *"Lā ilāha illa-Llāh,"* there is no *sajda* to be done except to Allah, and every time you say *"Lā ilāha illa-Llāh"* you will find yourself making *sajda* under the divine manifestation of His great, indescribable throne that you cannot see but which you feel. Each time you recite *"Lā ilāha illa-Llāh"* you are in *sajda*, physically and spiritually!

That is why they give you the daily *wird* to recite one-hundred to one-thousand times, *"Lā ilāha illa-Llāh."* We are not yet *awliyaullah*, but we imitate their footsteps; we cannot reach there, so we follow what they do. If we recite *"Lā ilāha illa-Llāh"* a thousand times, we are in *sajda* a thousand times!

Until Sayyidina 'Ubaydullah reached Maqām at-Tawhīd, each cell of his body was reciting *"Lā ilāha illa-Llāh,"* which means he remained in continuous *sajda*. That is why when you enter *sajda* you cannot raise your head! *Awliyaullah* remain in continuous *sajda* there, and from their respect they are never able to raise their heads or they are thrown out!

We make *sajda* like when chickens eat, quickly bobbing our heads up and down, not giving proper time and respect. Some people don't even stand erect after *ruku*, they go immediately into *sajda*. That is 'donkeyness'!

'Ubaydullah al-Amawi ؓ said, "I was not *muwahid*."

Sayyidina 'Abdul-Khāliq al-Ghujdawāni ؓ answered, "No, you were not, even with all the realities I opened to your heart. Now I will open for you Maqām at-Tawhīd."

The real *muwahid* is Sayyidina Muhammad ﷺ; all others are imitating him. Some are imitating him very well and they see the meaning of Maqām at-Tawhīd

After Sayyidina 'Abdul-Khāliq ؓ took 'Ubaydullah al-Amawi ؓ into that ocean which we cannot now describe, when you see where you are making *sajda*, you are in Maqām at-Tawhīd. At that time you will be given *imān* or else there is no faith, because everything before that was based on belief in the Unseen, and then you see it. When you see with those manifestations, you run away from it. That is why when a *wali* enters there he is locked with the beauty of what opened and where he reached. Then he opens Maqām at-Tawhīd, *shahādah* and the five pillars. After that he opens Maqām at-Imān, and then then Maqām at-Ihsān. The Shaykh has to take you through the reality of the entire *hadīth* that was related by Sayyidina 'Umar ﷺ.

Embracing the Six Articles of Faith

Every day we recite "*Lā ilāha illa-Llāh, Lā ilāha illa-Llāh*" many times, but we still have a problem with Maqām at-Tawhīd, which no one can deny. Anyone who says he has no problems does not understand the truth. Prophet ﷺ mentioned that even if you say *Lā ilāha illa-Llāh* with your tongue, you have committed hidden *shirk* by seeing yourself doing everything. *Ruyat un-nafs* is to see yourself as high, that you know everything. That is the problem with people, now and before.

Even presidents have the highest level of arrogance, which they show in debates with their political rivals. Everyone wants to be above the other. That is why it is better to find someone to lead you in submitting to Allah ﷻ as then no problem would arise, not here or in the Hereafter. They speak about foreign policy. When everyone is submitting, foreign policy would no longer be needed as everyone would know their limits, their borders and live in peace. There would be no more aggression as problems come from arrogance, from seeing the self as very high.

When we say, "*Lā ilāha illa-Llāh*," we are not saying it truthfully. Look at the Middle East; sorry to bring up an example from politics. Palestinians are asking to reclaim their occupied land, but they cannot live together. One group is fighting the other group, and for one year they were unable to reach an agreement. They throw each other in prison. Who will give them back their lands when they are fighting among themselves? You don't know who is responsible. However, if they submit, everyone will have trust. Therefore, to really say *Lā ilāha illa-Llāh* is to submit and trust in Allah ﷻ, rendering your problem to Him, then He will send peace and tranquility into your heart.

Everyone wants to be the boss and that is a problem. Why are people not reaching their aim, which is Allah's Divine Presence? Because no one is submitting to Allah ﷻ and each one wants to be higher than the other.

Awliyaullah know what shortcomings you have and they complete it for you and present it in the Divine Presence.

Sayyidina 'Abdul-Khāliq ق said, "Now I brought you to Maqām at-Tawhīd, and when you say *"Lā ilāha illa-Llāh,"* it means now your worship, the five pillars of Islam, are perfect. You are going to do them in the best way, because now these realities are opened to you." From that, Allah ﷻ took him to Maqām al-Imān, which, as everyone knows, is the first of the six Articles of Faith, *amantu billah,* "I believe in Allah."

When you say that, how then can you sin? When you feel you have belief in Allah ﷻ, it means you believe you are in His Sacred Presence. How can you then excuse yourself from that Presence? There is no absence at that point; you are always there, but in various levels or capacities.

So when you recite *amantu billah,* you should see yourself there. When you recite the second Pillar of Faith, *wa mala'ikati,* "and (I believe) in (His) angels," Allah ﷻ will give power for angels to help you, and He will give you power on angels—not all of them, but those dedicated to you—to work with them for your benefit and the benefit of those near you. However, now you tend to open the Holy Qur'an without even knowing the meaning of what you are reading.

The third Article of Faith is *wa kutubih,* "And (I believe) in (His) Holy Books." When you declare belief in Allah's Holy Books, He will open their secrets for you, in every letter 12,000 to 24,000 oceans of knowledge! More than that, when you recite the Holy Qur'an you will be able to see and understand the other Holy Books that Allah ﷻ sent the different Messengers.

The fourth Article of Faith is *wa rasūlih,* "And (I believe) in (His) Messengers." When you declare that, you will feel their presence in your life, like a loved ones' presence; if they are with you physically or not, you always feel them in front of your eyes. So if he loves you, how much do you think you would feel his presence? What do you think of one that Allah ﷻ and the Prophet ﷺ love best? You would be in the presence of those whom you love or who love you.

Then you move to Maqām al-Ihsān, where you will feel their presence. There, the Prophets will open from books given to them and show you some of the secrets they came with. It's not simple. *Tarīqah* is not a journey to a resort. When people go to a resort, they say, "O heavens!" Why do they compare it to heavens, because it is very beautiful and nice. Where men and women are naked is a heaven for them, but for you Heaven is the presence of the Prophets in your life.

In their biographies, *qisas al-anbiya*, "Stories of the Prophets," they will show you what they have done. You will feel it and live it from the secret of *imān*, from the faith they open for you at that level. Then Prophet ﷺ will open for you from his presence so that you always feel him in your life, because you are in love with him!

The fifth Article of Faith is, *wa yawm al-Ākhiri*, "and (I believe) in the Last Day."

The sixth Article of Faith is, *bi 'l qadr khayrihi wa sharrihi*, "and (I believe) in the predestination of good and evil." You have to believe in *qadr*, predestination, what is written or preordained. At that point, the struggle of believing or not believing ends and you see what *qadr* is written on. Until then, Allah ﷻ hid the Preserved Tablet from you, because if you saw what is destined you would not be able to live! You would see when and how you are going to die and all the problems arising in your life, and it would become difficult for you to bear. That is why the Preserved Tablet are open a little bit to the highest level *awliyaullah*.

The Coveted Ocean of Moral Excellence

When you establish these six Articles of Faith together with the Five Pillars of Islam, it takes you to Maqām al-Ihsān, the ocean of knowledge of good manners and moral excellence.

Sayyidina 'Abdul-Khāliq al-Ghujdawāni ق said to 'Ubaydullah al-Amawi ق, "O my son! I brought you all the way for all the promises you made to Prophet ﷺ and Allah ﷻ on the Day of Promises. I brought you at that moment to the reality that every *wali* dreams of: *tahaqqaq fihi jami' al-uhūd allatī akhadhaha min-Llāhi wa rasūlih*. 'Abdul-Khāliq ق brought all the covenants that Allah ﷻ and His Prophet ﷺ took from him, so he will see them, learn them, and follow them! They cannot reveal it because it is unique to each one; what is written for and granted to you is different than what is for others.

'Abdul-Khāliq ق said, "I am not leaving even one drop, because if even one drop of this ocean remains unopened it will become a problem for you. So I am opening every kind of covenant and promise that you gave to Allah ﷻ and His Prophet ﷺ. O My son! You have to know these are for you only and you must not share them with anyone. If you reveal the secret, they will take it from you. You cannot divulge secrets."

That is why Sayyidina Abu Hurayrah ﷺ said, "If I share with them what Prophet ﷺ taught me, they will cut my neck. I can share one kind of knowledge, but the other kind I cannot as it is only for me."

They would cut his neck because they cannot understand even from one *wali* to another. Each has his own guidance and knowledge that he perceives differently. That is why *murīds* of *awliyaullah* are different. Some people might come to Mawlana Shaykh Nazim ق, who is *Sultan al-Awliya* for us, but he might not like it and he may leave, because he is not one of Mawlana's spiritual children. He cannot stay; he has to go to someone else.

Awliyaullah do not look at *murīds* of others; it is *harām* for them. That is why you find two or three *awliya* or *khalīfahs* from the same Shaykh, but each one giving a different knowledge. To ask why each one is giving a different type of knowledge will put you at risk of opposing one or the other, so you must avoid that. Everyone has different knowledge.

Sayyidina 'Abdul-Khāliq ق said, "This is for you, but there are different verses in the Holy Qur'an for other people sitting here. There is unique guidance for each of them."

No *wali* is thinking about what his verse is. You probably never thought about it before. Their guidance is from their own, special verse that Allah ﷻ specified it on the Day of Promises.

The Holy Qur'an was revealed to Prophet ﷺ in *'Alam al-Arwah*, the World of Spirits, and then he revealed it to humanity. He said if all *awliya* put all their powers together to bring someone to his reality, they cannot, unless all *awliya* agree they will do that. There are 124,000 *awliya*, from the first level up to *Sultan al-Awliya*. If all their powers were brought together to bring one person to his own reality, they would not be able to do so except on that one condition. Even if they showed him how to pray, fast, and have good character and behavior, that *murīd* cannot reach his reality except on one condition.

Sayyidina 'Abdul-Khāliq al-Ghujdawāni ق, *Sultan al-Awliya* in his time, said, "They cannot reach their reality except through the verse Allah ﷻ dedicated to that servant on the Day of Promises. They must know in what verse their reality is embedded, then they can decode it and to bring out his reality through the door of that verse."

That is why everyone has a reality somewhere in the Holy Qur'an. That is one of the meanings of:

> *With Him are the keys of the Unseen, the treasures that no one knows but He. He knows whatever is on the earth and in the sea. Not a leaf falls but with His knowledge. There is not a grain in the darkness (or depths) of the earth, nor anything fresh or dry (green or withered), but is (inscribed) in a record clear (to those who can read).* (Surat al-An'ām, 6:59)

A *wali* is a living human being and we are like non-living beings, going to resorts, going to *dunya*, which for Allah has less value than a wing of a mosquito. You want to be living like Sayyidina al-Khidr, who found the Fountain of Youth, the Water of Life, *mai ul-hayyāt*. So "the living" want you to live; therefore, they must give.

Living and non-living beings are mentioned in the Holy Qur'an. Another meaning of *fi kitābin mubīn*, that everyone will have his own book on the Day of Judgment, which includes his own secrets. So *awliyaullah* go to those secrets found in the Holy Qur'an.

For this reason, you must be careful about what you say to others, especially in the presence of a *wali*, in the presence of the Prophet, or in the presence of Allah.

Wa Huwa ma' kum 'ayna mā kuntum.
And He is with you wherever you are. (Surat al-Hadīd, 57:4)

Luqman al-Hakīm said in one of his sayings, *wa inna min al-kalām maa Huwa ash-hadu min al-hajr*. "Be careful with what you speak; it is better to keep your mouth shut."

Don't talk, as Sayyidina 'Ali said, "Some words are harder than stone (rude) and more piercing than needles." One word is enough to make a war. *Wa amarru min as-sabr*, "and more bitter than the most sour." Sour is already bitter and some rude words are more bitter than sour. *Wa aharru min al-jamr*, "hotter than burning coal." *Wa inna min al-qulūbi maza'riun*, "On the other hand, there are hearts like farmlands." *f'azra'a fīhā 'l-kalimāt at-tayyibah fa in lam tanbut kulluha yanbut b'aduhā minhā*, "Plant in it the tree of good words." *Fa in lam yanbut kulluha, yanbut ba'duhā minhā*, "If all of it does not grow, some of it will grow." So make your heart a farmland where all trees are good ones. If all of it does not grow, some of it will grow and give you fruit.

Sayyidina 'Abdul-Khāliq al-Ghujdawāni ق said, "O my son! This is my advice to you now, which Allah ﷻ has opened to you from your own private verse of guidance. But you have to know that all the other verses of the Holy Qur'an are surely going to save you from Hellfire, from punishment."

It means anyone who reads them will be saved from punishment; however, your door to reach reality is through that one verse. Don't forget that the Holy Qur'an is the Holy Word of Allah ﷻ that will save you and humanity from any difficulty and problem!

Therefore, those who want to reach their destinies and the secrets of the Holy Qur'an must go through the verse that is written for them, and there is no way you can reach it except from the spring or source that is dedicated to you. Even if you spent the lifespan of Sayyidina Nuh ؑ, a thousand years in prayer, seclusions, and worship, you would not reach guidance or gain other than exhaustion and hardship, because your guidance is wrapped in the *nur* of that *ayah*.

So it means that what is given to one is not given to another. If we understood that we wouldn't fight, because everyone has his own 'way'. Don't worry too much, for what is written will occur. It is not you who decides: it has been decided for you.

Can your child decide for himself or herself, or do you decide for them? Why don't you leave young children to decide? You decide for them or they might fatally injure themselves. So Allah ﷻ has decided for His servants because no one can reach maturity except through *awliyaullah*, by the *barakah* of Sayyidina Muhammad ﷺ. So until you reach maturity, you cannot decide.

After exhausting yourself for a thousand years, you will find you need a teacher to give you your verse, the code for your door, to reach your destiny. That is what we are looking for, so don't worry too much. What is written will happen. So submit to Allah ﷻ as submission will take you everywhere!

There Are No Questions in Tariqah!

As more knowledge comes more questions arise, unless you submit completely to Allah ﷻ as Prophet ﷺ submitted. He never asked one question; he waited for the answer to come in divine revelation.

Sayyidina Musa ﷺ is an example. Whatever level of knowledge he reached, the more questions he asked. Through him, Allah is teaching *ummat an-Nabi* ﷺ. That is to show the difference of other Messengers and the Seal of Messengers ﷺ. That is why Sayyidina Khidr ﷺ said to Sayyidina Musa ﷺ, "You cannot have patience with me. Whatever I do you will question."

That big scholar, 'Ubaydullah al-Amawi ق, questioned, "When Allah offered us *uhūd* (duties we pledged on the Day of Promises), who among us said, 'Yes'? Is it the *rūh* mentioned in the verse, *wa nafakhtu fihi min rūhī*, "I breathed into him of My spirit." (38:72) Is it *qudrah,* the secret of al-Khāliq, Who creates that ocean from endless oceans? Where is that from and who answered? What is that *rūh*?"

Why ask? Do you want to show you know something? Wait until Allah ﷻ opens it!

He continued, "Or is it the *rūh* the two angels blow into the womb of the mother after four months of pregnancy? Or is it the *rūh* in the 366 energy points of human beings, that makes those points work together in symmetry? Or is it the *rūh* that Allah put between *dunya* and *Ākhirah* when a person dies, in 'Alam al-Barzakh, the world between *dunya* and *Ākhirah*? What kind of *rūh* is in the grave? After all these different *rūh,* I am asking which one answered on the Day of Promises? Is it all of them, or one of them? If they answered, does it means they have an existence, and if so, what kind of existence? Is it a combination of worldly and heavenly existence? If so, what combines them?"

Such questions came to Sayyidina 'Ubaydullah al-Amawi ق; even after they answered, he asked more questions!

"About the combination of different *rūh*, did Allah take back that power He gave that *rūh* to answer, leaving it deceased? If so, where did they die, in heavens? They are not in earth. If they died they don't exist anymore, so where are they and what is the name of that level? If Allah put them in a certain level in Paradise, what is that level where they await their turn to come to *dunya*? That is my question for that period."

Sayyidina 'Abdul-Khāliq al-Ghujdawāni ق said, "O my son! That is too many questions. Are there more questions on the next level?"

Sayyidina 'Ubaydullah said, *"Ya Sayyidi,* I have too many questions."

That means no one knows the Unseen except Allah. Don't try to dig, like the People of Musa ﷺ, when Allah ordered them to slaughter a cow. They asked so many questions!

"Where can we find that cow? How old is it? What color is it? What kind of cow is it" From their questioning, that command became very complicated to fulfill. They searched everywhere until they found one cow with that narrow description. Do you know how they found it?

> *And lo! Moses said unto his people, "Behold! God bids you to sacrifice a cow." They said, "Do you mock at us?" He answered, "I seek refuge with God against being so ignorant!" They said, "Pray on our behalf to your Sustainer that He makes clear to us what she is to be like." (Moses) replied, "Behold, He says it is to be a cow neither old nor immature, but of an age in-between. Do then what you have been ordered!" They said, "Pray on our behalf to your Sustainer that He makes clear to us what her color should be." (Moses) answered, "Behold! He says it is to be a yellow cow, bright of hue, pleasing to the beholder." They said, "Pray on our behalf to your Sustainer that He makes clear to us what she is to be like, for to us all cows resemble one another; then, if God so wills, we shall truly be guided aright!" (Moses) answered, "Behold! He says it is to be a cow not broken in to plow the earth or to water the crops, free of fault, without markings of any other color." They said, "At last you brought out the truth!" And thereupon they sacrificed her, although they had almost left it undone.* (Surat al-Baqara, 2:67-71)

Their questions could fill a journal! What do you think about the questions 'Ubaydullah asked about the trust and the *rūh*? *Dunya* will end before the complete answers are known! When the People of Musa ﷺ began to make difficulties, Allah made the order more complicated. Eventually they found the cow. Someone said, "When I was taking my goats on Mount Ararat, a very high mountain, I saw a very old lady."

We don't know how old that was, perhaps hundreds of years old. Then they had to send someone all the way to Ararat from Jerusalem to find that cow. They found that lady and asked, "How old are you?"

She said, "I don't know. I remember it raining on that mountain day and night until water rose up the mountain." It means she was from time of Sayyidina Nuh ﷺ. If Allah wants to save anything, He will! That is why in the time of Sayyidina Mahdi ﷺ, the Last Day will not come until a big war breaks out and a big explosion occurs in front of you, and you are saved by Allah's Will.

They found that cow, which was preserved from the time of Sayyidina Nuh ﷺ! So they asked the owner, "Can we get it?"

The cow's owner answered, "No, that is my only cow."

"What can we give you in exchange?" they asked.

"One-thousand cows!"

Where could they get one-thousand cows? They were going to refuse Sayyidina Musa's ﷺ order because they were stingy.

For those who are patient in their lives, you don't know what Allah ﷻ will reward at the end. Be patient, because you cannot see future, so surrender to Allah's Will! Allah rewarded that lady with one-thousand cows for that one cow, which they slaughtered.

Once in 1967 in our home in Beirut, Mawlana Shaykh Nazim ق was explaining something and this verse of Holy Qur'an came to his heart:

Fa li kullin wijhun Huwa muwaliha fastabiqū al-khayrāt.
To each is a goal to which Allah turns him; then strive together (as in a race).
(Surat al-Baqara, 2:148)

It means Allah ﷻ puts everyone in a specific direction, so compete for good. Everyone has a way to follow in his life. You cannot say, "I want this," or, "I want that." Whatever is in your direction you will get, like a train on track, so you will see what is there. You cannot jump to someone else's track. Allah ﷻ accepted your promise that you will follow that direction and no other.

Mawlana Shaykh said, "I am not the one to answer. That question must be asked of Grandshaykh when you go to Shām as he knows the secret of that verse."

I was asking, like all of us today, "O *Sayyidi*! Where is my trust? What is my real name? What kind turban should I put?" Too many questions!

I was very anxious to reach Damascus, and went up to Grandshaykh's room and asked the question. He looked at me and didn't answer, and I knew he was not happy. So then I said, "Mawlana Shaykh told me to ask you." I threw it on Mawlana!

Grandshaykh ق said, "There is Grand Mufti in Damascus who can answer your question. Go to him and ask. Here is *tarīqah*. Here you sit with *adab*. Come and wait for the order."

I never saw anyone come to Grandshaykh ق and say, "I have this burden." They came, took *barakah,* and went. Now people come to Mawlana Shaykh and unload, "I have this problem and this problem...." Ask him to pray for you, which is enough because he already knows! It will be more effective for your problem.

So Grandshaykh ق said, "Here is spirituality." It means, *awliya* don't like followers to ask questions, especially in matters of knowledge. They open for you what you can take and not more. The mind always likes to take more, but the heart is not ready, like in the case of 'Ubaydullah al-Amawi ق. When the answer comes, you will know, like when my uncle wanted to ask about Allah's Greatest Name and Grandshaykh ق brought the answer without him asking; then he knew it was a miracle!

When 'Ubaydullah al-Amawi ق asked so many questions, Sayyidina 'Abdul-Khāliq al-Ghujdawāni ق said, "Oh my son! If you had looked at me with submission you would never need to ask."

It means, "Although I put you in that level you are not yet ready to know the reality, because you are not yet fully submitting to me."

When Sayyidina Abdul-Wahhab ash-Shara'ani ق was asked about *'Ilm al-Bātin*, Hidden Knowledge, and *'Ilm al-Dhāhir*, Apparent Knowledge. He said, "We don't have hidden and apparent knowledge. We have already seen the hidden knowledge that became apparent, so we have only one knowledge, that of reality."

Many times we told the story of Sayyidina Ahmad al-Badawi ق, who often asked, "O Allah! Open You door for me." Finally submitted to that *wali*, who took all his scholarly knowledge. After that, all he knew was that he was on the right track, and he submitted to the Shaykh. After a while the Shaykh reappeared and poured real knowledge into his heart, so that he was satisfied and had no need to ask questions.

Sayyidina 'Abdul-Khāliq al-Ghujdawāni ق said, "*Ya* 'Ubaydullah! You didn't take the key when he came to you, because you did not submit. Submit now or I will not give it." At that moment 'Ubaydullah al-Amawi ق found himself in complete annihilation of the Shaykh, in complete submission, a state in which he received knowledge without asking any questions.

Shaykh 'Abdul-Khāliq ق said, "I opened this to prevent you from falling into the difficulties Ahmad al-Badawi ق fell into. I don't want you in *ta'b;* I want your complete submission."

About Those Who Accepted the Trust

When Allah ﷻ offered the trust the heavens, earth and mountains said, "We cannot accept it." Angels in heavens said, "O our Lord! That is difficult!"

> *Truly, We offered al-Amānah (the Trust) to the heavens and the earth, and the mountains, but they declined to bear it and were afraid of it, but Man bore it. Verily, he was unjust (to himself) and ignorant (of its results).*
>
> (Surat al-Ahzāb, 33:72)

When someone entrusts something to you, even for ten or fifteen years, even if your children are dying, you cannot use it without permission. When offered the Trust, angels said, "Leave us as we are; we are worshipping." Then Allah offered the Trust to the earth, which said, "That is too heavy on me. I cannot take it." earth carries countless creatures on it, and yet is always praising Allah ﷻ. However, it declined. Then Allah offered the Trust to the mountains (which means *anbiyaullah* and *awliyaullah*), but they were worried and also declined. Only mankind said, "Yes, we will take it!" *innahu kāna zhalūman jahūla*, "He was ignorant and oppressive."

He said, "I will give you those when Allah offered that *amānah*, who answered and accepted it. What was that 'Essence,' if we can call it that, which accepted to take that trust? If someone knows, it means he will combine himself in *dunya* with that Essence or *rūh!*"

This is a very complex line of questioning, which means, "If you combine yourself with that, you will know Allah ordered us, and you promised to do that in *dunya*." It is important to understand, this is where *awliyaullah* connect their students.

'Ubaydullah al-Amawi ق is asking Shaykh 'Abdul-Khāliq ق to explain who answered Allah ﷻ on the Day of Promises and are they still there waiting to come to *dunya*, or did Allah ﷻ cause them to die and then live? Are they dead there, or are they still there glorifying Allah ﷻ?

Sayyidina 'Abdul-Khāliq al-Ghujdawāni ق said, "O my son! You are unable to grasp this reality because it is above your current level. The reality of what answered Allah ﷻ cannot be described by human tongues. Spiritual knowledge belongs to heavens and Allah ﷻ released it to Prophet ﷺ in Mi'rāj and there is no language to describe what Prophet ﷺ gave to *awliyaullah* and therefore, whatever I tell you, you are not going to understand it."

What if I tell you there is a precious stone more valuable than diamonds? You will not understand it as it doesn't exist, so there is no language to express it. *Al-ma'dūm, al-nādiru ka 'l-ma'dūm*, "Tell them, don't tell me (about things that are rare, as if they don't exist)." You cannot say what is rare exists. That is what he wants to tell him, that Reality is rare and does not exist in *dunya*; it exists for heavens but not for earth. So whatever I am going to speak to you on my tongue will be according to *dunya and* cannot be from the level of *Ākhirah*. It means, "Since you asked me a physical question I am giving you an answer that relates to that physical question." That might give you an understanding that for you is a drop of an ocean, but still that drop is okay, still good.

So he said, "What we can say is, what answered there is something that is the origin from which Allah ﷻ created the Reality of human beings."

Allah ﷻ created:

Khalaqah 'l-insāna min salsālin ka 'l-fakhkhār.
Allah created human beings from sounding clay like (used for) pottery.
(Surat ar-Rahmān, 55:14-15)

"*Salsāl*" is a sauce that is empty like clay used in pottery making, and like clay, Allah ﷻ created human beings from a heavenly mud that He ﷻ originally created from a single cell. Today scientists say one-cell creatures "evolved," but from what? That confuses them and they cannot go beyond it, asking, "What is that?" Allah ﷻ created creation from one cell, what *awliyaullah* refer to as "*adh-dharrah*" after "*dharr*," the Arabic word for "ant," the smallest creature people understood at that time.

He said, "Not *dharrah* alone, but in combination." The *dharrah* has no life, but it is the origin of creation and part of human beings. When Allah ﷻ said *nafakhtu fīhi min rūhī*, "When I blow from that Beautiful Name, (al-Khāliq)." He blows from that Divine Name into that cell, which is the origin of human beings and every human being has a different cell. Although all are created from one cell, the reality of that Essence is a combination of all cells to come in the future.

If you put too many atoms near each other it becomes big, but in that, Allah ﷻ is not making that cell bigger or smaller. It includes all the cells and still it is an atom, the smallest particle to exist but not getting bigger. So that heavenly Essence that Allah created first, who is that? It is the reality of Sayyidina Muhammad ﷺ, from which everything appeared! So when Allah want to put that Reality from the Beautiful Name "al-Khāliq," He has to put it in something clean. Who was the perfect, highest, blessed, clean one? Who was in that lamp?

The Atom of Sayyidina Muhammad's Creation

The Perfect One ﷺ was under the gaze of Allah ﷻ for 70,000 years, raising him higher and higher in knowledge, raising his Essence. Allah will not put that light that He is sending into that atom if it is not clean in *dunya*. And that was reality of Sayyidina Muhammad ﷺ that Allah sent one drop of *Bahr al-Qudrah* from the ocean of the Creator to the Ocean of Power. *Min ismAllah al-Khāliq ila ismAllah al-Qādir*, "From the Beautiful Name 'al-Khāliq' to the Beautiful Name 'al-Qadir,' He sent that reality. That is the meaning of:

> *Wa nafakhtu fīhī min rūhī.*
> *And breathed into him of My Spirit.* (Suratu al-Hijr, 15:29)

What many scholars interpret as, "I blow My *Rūh* in him," is one of the meanings that Sayyidina 'Abdul-Khāliq al-Ghujdawāni ق explains on the tongues of *awliya*. He said, "It is the Essence and Reality of Sayyidina Muhammad ﷺ, that *dharrah*, atom, was able to have all other atoms in it without it being bigger or smaller, and the Light that entered that atom—the combination of that Light and the Essence of Prophet ﷺ–answered on behalf of every one before this universe was created. Allah knows when, but on the Day of Promises that Essence answered when Allah ﷻ asked, *'alastu bi-rabbikum.'*"

Just as the body needs the soul in order to move the reality of Sayyidina Muhammad ﷺ in the reality of everyone that is in that cell, needed in that atom needed that, these two Beautiful Names from the ocean of the Beautiful Name al-Khāliq to the ocean of the Name al-Qadir, that

Light was moving and the combination of that Light with the Essence of the Prophet answered, "*Ya Rabbī*! You are The One to be worshipped." And the trust was given to that one, because no one can carry the trust except Sayyidina Muhammad ﷺ. That is why in *Laylat al-Isrā' wa 'l-Mi'rāj* when he reached *Qāba Qawsayni wa Adnā*, Allah ﷻ showed him the reality of all the *dharrāt*, Bani Adam that are coming from him, stored in the Reality of Sayyidina Muhammad ﷺ.

> *W 'alamū anna fīkum Rasūlullah.*
> And know that the Messenger of Allah is in you.   (Surat al-Hujurat, 49:7)

The Light of Muhammad ﷺ is in everyone and without it no one can move. "The light of every human being is from those three Lights. The first Light is from Allah's Beautiful Name "al-Khāliq" to the Beautiful Name "al-Qadir." The second Light is from the reality of:

> *Wa man arsalanāka illa rahmatan li 'l-'ālamīn.*
> We sent you not (O Muhammad) except as Mercy to all creation.
> (Surat al-Anbiya, 21:107)

The Light coming from Prophet ﷺ is the Light of the Reality of Human Beings that comes from Sayyidina Adam ﷺ. On the Day of *Isrā' wa 'l-Mi'rāj*, Allah said to Prophet ﷺ, "*Ya* Muhammad! I give you the *ummah* as a trust. Do you accept?" and Allah ﷻ showed them to him at their highest level of worshipness, very clean, without sins, and Prophet ﷺ was so happy to see all creation in that state.

But when Allah ﷻ gave them to Prophet ﷺ, how were they clean? It means you were in the state of complete worshipness, and from that day your atom appeared in Prophet ﷺ within *Muhammadun Rasūlullah:* from that day until you came into *dunya* you were worshipping without sin, until the day you came to your mother's womb. That's why you are born on *fitra*. So when Allah ﷻ showed him high-worshipping human beings, Prophet ﷺ was very happy and said, "*Ya Rabbī*, I accept!" and Allah said, "Give them back clean as I gave them to you."

Then Allah ﷻ showed him what they are going to do in *dunya*, that all of them will become dirty, whereas originally they were all clean. From outside you are exposed as dirty, but you are two-sided: one side is clean, one side is dirty. Between the two is a veil, so that dirty side cannot contaminate the clean one. There is a veil that blocks one side from the other.

> *Maraj al-bahrayni yaltaqiyan, baynahuma barzakhun lā yabghiyan.*
>
> *He let forth the two seas so that they meet together (but) between them is a barrier that they do not transgress.* (Surat ar-Rahmān, 55: 19,20)

SubhanAllah! They say the Atlantic and the Mediterranean Oceans cannot mix because between them is a barrier. Good and bad cannot mix, there is a barrier. So Allah said to Prophet, "*Ya* Muhammad! That is why I created an *ummah* that never tires of sinning. I am their Lord, and I never tire of forgiving them." That side is clean and between these two oceans of the good and the bad there is a barrier: that is why what is good is good forever, and what is bad, Allah doesn't look at it.

What Answered Allah on the Day of Promises?

In an atom you have the mass and the electrons, and without electrons that atom is dead completely. The smallest essence, the origin of the human being or creation, is that atom which has that drop of Reality from the Ocean of Existence, and let's say it makes human beings alive. So what answered Allah on the Day of Promises is the Reality with that drop of existence that has been given to Prophet. Atoms of all other creations are under the control of Prophet and are within his existence, which is why he was created first as these atoms need the Light of Sayyidina Muhammad. And the meaning of the Light of Sayyidina Muhammad is the drop of existence that Allah put in the atom of Prophet, and that Light is from different lights that went to different atoms.

So the one that answered is the one in whose ocean all other atoms are swimming! After they answered, with all of them in the answer of the Prophet, Allah put all those atoms that were to come to *dunya* in *Barzakh bayn al-Jannah wa 'dh-Dhuhūr*. There is another *barzakh* we live in between our death and resurrection, and there was a *barzakh* from the time they answer within Prophet until they appear in *dunya* where it is not Paradise and not in-between, because Paradise is not given until *taklīf*, when you are given the responsibility of worship. After that, Paradise exists. It is not a precondition to enter Paradise, although. Paradise has a condition to enter it, which is the responsibility of accepting worship, or we can say when you worship, you then deserve Paradise.

'Abdul-Khāliq ق answered that *murīd*, saying Allah ﷻ put them in a place that is not Paradise and not other than Paradise. *Awliyaullah* say they were in the existence of Sayyidina Muhammad. *li anna Allah harām al-jannah hatta ba'd at-taklīf*, "Allah prohibited to enter Paradise until taking responsibility of worship." So don't say, "I am going to enter Paradise without worship." You might believe in Allah ﷻ and Prophet ﷺ and you could enter as you have belief, but you have not worshipped, and judgment is reserved for Allah ﷻ.

It is important to know, that atom has been saved. Allah ﷻ does not need a freezer to save it as they do today; that atom has a portion of that Light from that drop inside it that cannot appear in *dunya* without the blowing of the two angels into in mother's womb after four months. That sperm, if we want to call it that, is among millions of sperm but only one carries the secret and when it touches the egg it then goes into complete formation. If all the millions of other sperm touch the egg, nothing will happen; only that one designated sperm has to touch, and that will not happen without the order of those two angels that are waiting, watching and navigating that sperm like a spaceship to that egg to fertilize each other.

That process is to show Allah's Greatness, in creating millions of sperm every time, but only one of them is navigated millions of miles or kilometers in comparison to its size and through many obstacles, until they reach the egg that has the secret. Even when the corresponding egg and sperm finally connect, if the final blowing doesn't come from angels it doesn't come to *dunya*; rather, it dissolves.

By Allah's Order, those angels are waiting to know if they will send the *rūh*—the Light and its secret—or not? So when the two angels blow, on that level it is called "*ar-rūh*," the Spirit, and you cannot describe it as being from Allah's "Soul." Allah gives the order to the two angels and they order the combination of atom and Light, the mass, to hit the egg and form a new child that will appear in *dunya*. Furthermore, the angels are working on that *dharrah* all the way to its maturity. Boy or girl, angels develop the physicality of that human being: its height, coloring, how its ears will be, what type of body it will have, all is in the power of those angels. As that person reaches maturity, his reality will understand that he is responsible for the oath he took on the Day of Promises. That is why a child is not responsible until he or she reaches maturity.

Until then, that atom remains in *Barzakh*, from the Day of Promises until its appearance in *dunya*. Just as Allah ﷻ said, "Oh fire, be cool and peaceful on Ibrāhīm," that *Barzakh* is a heavenly freezer that preserves you in your purest state and you don't have to worry until you come to *dunya*.

The Three Realities of Every Human Being

Sayyidina 'Abdul-Khāliq ق said, "*Ya* 'Ubaydullah! Now you reached the *yaqīn*, certainty of understanding what I said. Had you a drop of real submission from the beginning you would not have asked questions, but we deprived you of reaching that submission so you would ask questions and others will get the answers. Now your questions finished and I am going to explain something. Every human being has three main realities, *haqa`iq*. First is *adh-dharrah*, the reality of the essence of the human being, which is inanimate atom that does not move. Second is the essence of that drop of Light in it from *wa nafakhtu fīhi min rūhī* that makes it to move. Third is *al-hayyat*, the immediate life blown into it by those two angels. It will go through these three processes."

Shaykh 'Abdul-Khāliq Ghujdawāni ق had not finished speaking when 'Ubaydullah al-Amawi ق asked another question, because as they ascended more questions came to his heart. He asked, "My Master! How are you able to speak about the Hidden Unseen Realities from the past and from the future, because if you speak from the future, if Allah changes '*yamhullah ma yashau wa yuthbit wa indahu ummul-kitāb,*' what you said will become incorrect. So what you can say, O my master?" He is put his master in a corner.

'Ubaydullah is asking about a complex issue! That is precisely why *awliyaullah* say, "Mahdi is coming tomorrow," or, "after forty days," or, "after one year." It was written that he will come in forty days, but Allah ﷻ changed it. So 'Ubaydullah al-Amawi ق asked, "How do *awliyaullah* say things about the past and future if Allah changes it?"

How we can explain this? If someone died and punishment was written for him, but Allah ﷻ changed the outcome to put him in Paradise, what are you going to say when his reality is now in *Jannah*, as Allah ﷻ said in Holy Qur'an, *kullu yawmin Huwa fī shān*, "Every day He attends to a different affair," which means that Allah ﷻ owns that day, so if He changes it or not is up to Him.

Now his master became tough and replied, "O my son," still giving respect. "Listen well and understand what I am going to say as this is a lesson for everyone. A *murīd* went to his Shaykh, who was a big *wali*, and asked, 'O my Shaykh! Do I need to take *bay'a* to follow you, although I know by heart all knowledges in the four *madhāhib*? Ask any question you want and I will answer. Also, Allah gave me power to know what is in Eight Heavens and complete knowledge of everything that exists there. I know all the realities under the *'Arsh* and down. I know the graves of every prophet, where each is buried and its places. I listen to and can hear the glorification of all creation, including animals and the fish in the ocean, and I know the secret of, "Wa *in min shay'in illa yusabihu bihamdihi*, and there is not a thing but celebrates His praise!' (17:44) I move in space by the power of *tayy* and I see how *awliyaullah* visit each other. I know all the secrets of the *āhadīth* that Prophet ﷺ opened to me. I have memorized the entire Holy Qur'an with a secret to it, and I know how to interpret it. Do I need a *murshid* when I have all these knowledges? With all that I have, do I need anything?'"

Sayyidina 'Abdul-Khāliq ق is telling 'Ubaydullah, "With all I have, do you still have questions? This one is higher than you by far and yet you ask if you need a *murshid*?" Then he said, "Oh my son! Let us say what you said is correct and we believe it. However, I am going to ask you something and if you know it, I will accept what you say and if you don't know it, I will reject what you say," inferring, "You need a *murshid* even if you have all these knowledges because you still have ego, so are you ready?" This gives us an idea that *awliyaullah* have egos, depending on their levels.

Then 'Ubaydullah trembled, thinking, "The Shaykh is going to ask me a question? Will he fail me even though I have all these knowledges?"

Or here, is 'Ubaydullah going to become the *murshid*? He did not surrender and continued to ask questions, because they push the higher *wali* to get more out of him. One *wali* is fishing with a pole, catching one after one, and the other is fishing with a big net, taking thousands of fish at a time. 'Abdul-Khāliq ق was fishing with a big net.

He told 'Ubaydullah, "I will ask you one question, and remember, '*la'n Allah al-kadhibīn*, Allah cursed the liars,' so answer truthfully."

But let's consider that if someone really has that much knowledge, what does he want with Sayyidina 'Abdul-Khāliq ق? Can anyone say, "I memorized the entire Holy Qur'an and its meaning," when the meaning of Holy Qur'an never ends? Can you go to Mawlana Shaykh Nazim ق and say, "I have knowledge from *'Arsh* and below, I move in space and I hear the *tasbih* of all creation." If that were the case, you would establish your own shrine! If Allah ﷻ opened as He did to 'Ubaydullah al-Amawi ق, for anyone to claim that is a sickness in the heart. So 'Ubaydullah thought to himself, "I know this much," but the Shaykh wanted to demolish his ego and arrogance.

Sayyidina 'Ubaydullah ق spoke at length, trying to teach Sayyidina 'Abdul-Khāliq al-Ghujdawāni ق, who listened, because *awliyaullah* submit to the order of Allah ﷻ and when anyone comes they listen. That is the order of Sayyidina 'Āli, *al-istima,* "listen," then move. We move before we listen or hear anything and we also speak, but first you must listen, then move, and do not take decisions quickly or it will destroy you.

Who is *al-'aqal*, the sober one, and who is *al-majnūn*, the crazy one? The crazy one rejects whatever comes to him, without listening. If such a one tells you a hundred times, "I say this and believe what I am saying," don't believe him! Also, when husband and wife quarrel both are crazy and during such arguments don't bring up what happened one hour ago or angels will curse you! Grandshaykh ق said, "Don't bring up what happened one hour ago as it is gone. Live in this moment." Why? Because *Shaytan* wants to bring back what happened previously only to make you angry and that will destroy you.

As Sayyidina 'Āli said, "Be quiet." Say to yourself, "*Ya* Allah! I am your servant and I am bad. You put that one on me to polish my character." If you do that, you will be granted moral excellence and Prophet ﷺ will gaze at you, but not when you don't accept others. So we must think, "*Ya Rabbī!* You sent that one to talk and teach me."

That is the first level in *tarīqah*. If I beat someone, immediately he will rebel against me, but in *tarīqah* he doesn't even have the right to look back to see who beat him. If your wife looked at you and said something, don't look back and answer or she will become more upset, and even if she made you upset you must not answer. If she shouts, "You are not answering me!" then we know *Shaytan* entered.

How do you answer a drunk person? Police use a 'breathalyzer' to measure a person's blood alcohol level; do you think angels are not measuring and checking? Any word that comes from your mouth that is not from the way of Allah and Qur'an is considered dirt from the toilet! So 'Ubaydullah al-Amawi ق arrogantly told his Shaykh, "I see this and this and this," so arrogance comes back on him. So if someone hit you, keep moving and don't look back.

The Wrestler Who Took His Trust

You heard the story of the wrestler who came to Grandshaykh ق. When you take *tarīqah* it is like getting married; you bring someone new into your home. Like a watermelon with both red and white flesh, you have to eat it or else why did you decide to buy it? If you won't eat it because you found something you don't like, it is better not to buy it but to just say, "I don't want to eat watermelon," and keep to yourself!

So he came to the Shaykh with a dagger and gun, and his turban sideways on his head, covering one eye, and he said, "Shaykh, I want *tarīqah*!" If someone comes like a gangster, what would you say? But the Shaykh saw his heart is pure. Similarly, when a couple marries their hearts are pure, but *Shaytan* will try to destroy the happy relationship. Allah ﷻ is so happy when they make peace, because *Shaytan*'s back will break from it as he never likes people to reunite!

So the Shaykh sent the wrestler to three people; first to a person carrying all kinds of sheep intestines, saying, "Go beat him on his neck."

The wrestler was happy and said, "Okay, I'll beat him up!"

He found the first one and beat him on his neck, and the intestines flew everywhere. That one looked at the wrestler with anger, as if to say, "O my teacher! I know you sent me that one to test me, but I don't joke with me like that." He is a beginner. The wrestler told the Shaykh what happened.

The Shaykh said, "Never mind, I'll send you to another one tomorrow. Now you sleep." And the next day he sent him to another one to beat him up and the wrestler beat him hard until he fell on the floor. That one looked at him and smiled, as if to say, "Oh my Shaykh! I know you sent him and it is okay with me." When anyone fights, it means they are not submitting to Allah and the angels are cursing them. When husbands and wives fight, they often bring stories from the past. So *tarīqah* is not at all easy when you examine the discipline required to make progress. You cannot play with the discipline and without it, you cannot enter even the first step!

Awliya have a spiritual whip and because we are donkeys, they ride us and use the whip. You know the donkey, he took a decision, "I am not moving even if you whip me a hundred times! You are stubborn and I am stubborn. I cannot move from the point I decided." Too many wives and husbands are like that, but we say it is better to try to be lenient when she is stubborn, don't you also be stubborn. At that moment, loosen it up. If he is being stubborn, loosen it up and then he will move, just like the donkey will eventually move. Check yourself, if you are not able to move to a new chapter as that is 'donkeyness'.

So that one looked, smiling arrogantly, as if to say, "I know your tricks." So the next day he sent ʿUbaydullah al-Amawi ق to a farmer and said, "Break your stick on his back." That farmer was plowing his field with an ox, and ʿUbaydullah beat him, but the man didn't look back, he just pushed harder on the plow for the ox to move faster. ʿUbaydullah hit him a second time, and again he pushed harder on the plow to move faster. He hit him a third time, the stick broke, and that man ran to him and said, "Please, on the Day of Judgment don't come against me because I injured your hand from beating me!" That is a *murīd*. Can you do that? How far are we from being *murīds*? We are still crawling, not yet walking.

So the Shaykh said to the wrestler, "The first one is a beginner, the second one is ready and the third one is *a murīd*." Then he took the wrestler to a garden and told him, "See this apple tree? With all your power, take this stone and throw it at that apple tree."

He threw it and ten apples fell down and the branch cracked.

He said, "O my son! You have to be like that tree. If someone harmed you and cracked you, even crushed you down or wounded you, you still have to give him ten apples because for every good action Allah gives ten *hasanat*, so the tree gave ten. So be a fruit tree and don't be *Shaytan*."

Immediately he built up that wrestler to be with the Prophet ﷺ in three days, because he was so sincere. Also the other one, ʿUbaydullah al-Amawi ق, was sincere, but had he not asked all those questions we would not be able to learn from it.

We must learn that in this life there is no permission to come against one another. We must be like sheep: after a little while they make a sound and they know their duty. After Fajr, they move in a line outside and go to the field to eat grass. They never look up. Who is like that? Human beings are arrogant. Sheep are like that, looking to where they are going to put their feet and moving. They don't bite each other, they are happy with each other and in the evening coming back as if coming from the mosque. Allah ﷻ will build such a person a palace each time he goes and comes, which means going and coming with submission, never looking up, always looking down! Be sheep and look down while walking, you will get miracles! *SubhanAllah*, in the evening they come back. Be like that; go sweet and come back sweet, don't go sour and come back sour.

So 'Abdul-Khāliq al-Ghujdawāni ق said, "O my son! All that you said doesn't make sense to me. Knowledge of *sajda* under *'Arsh* and down, knowing about holy Prophets, knowing Holy Qur'an and knowing *tasbih* of every creation will not take you anywhere. That will save you from Hellfire and take you to Paradise, but with such knowledge, it is impossible to give you what you are seeking."

Today if you only know the alphabet, you think you are an *'ālim*. What do you think about a scholar who memorized Qur'an and *hadīth*? Then no one can pull him down because he is glued to the chair!

The Shaykh, 'Abdul-Khāliq al-Ghujdawāni ق, said, "All the knowledge you have is full of moths that will eat it. Drop that luggage you are bringing and come."

'Ubaydullah al-Amawi ق said, "How to drop it? I spent decades to fill it up."

'Abdul-Khāliq al-Ghujdawāni ق said, "All you built is filled with moths. Come and build it clean, as if you know nothing."

'Ubaydullah answered, "O Shaykh! Don't say this in front of people. Everyone knows I am Shaykh al-Islam."

"What Shaykh al-Islam? You are arrogant, therefore you are Shaykh ash-*Shaytan*, asking all these questions of the Shaykh. You need a purifier."

"Where I can get that purifier, *ya Sayyidi*? Like Ahmad al-Badawi ق, I am ready to give up all my knowledge and be a servant at your door."

'Abdul-Khāliq ق said, "I have many servants and all of them like to serve me!" He is poking him, downsizing his ego, cutting the peacock's feathers.

Finally, 'Ubaydullah answered, "O my Shaykh! What must I do?"

'Abdul-Khāliq ق said, "Accept me."

'Ubaydullah thought, "Accept me as a donkey at your door," humbling himself.

'Abdul-Khāliq al-Ghujdawāni ق said, "All of these you see are donkeys and I ride on them. They accept whatever I say, so I don't need another donkey here."

'Ubaydullah thought, "What must I say to the Shaykh to get him to accept me? To be a donkey means 'dress me with patience because I am too ignorant to understand it.' This is not enough?" Finally he said, "O my Shaykh! Accept me as dog at your door."

The Shaykh said, "All of these are dogs at my door. of them bark. I don't need more dogs."

'Ubaydullah al-Amawi ق didn't know what else to say, but, *"Ya Sayyidi*! I will eat all their garbage and take them to their destinies, and carry their burdens and come to you, come to Prophet ﷺ, and come to Allah's Door with them, all clean." He was powerful to do that and he was sincere.

'Abdul-Khāliq al-Ghujdawāni ق said, said, "O my son! Of all you said, I accept the last one, as no one tried to be that. But to achieve that you must throw all your questions in the ocean. With all your knowledge that you spoke of, with all that *kashf* and visions, you must answer one question and submit to me."

'Ubaydullah replied, "I will answer, O my Shaykh, and will tell you the truth. With all these knowledges, still I don't feel content and I am not capable of knowing what is missing. That is why I asked all these questions. Whatever different oceans I enter or whatever different visions I experience, I am still not content, but I am trying my best and that is why I came to you."

'Abdul-Khāliq al-Ghujdawāni ق recited the verse of Holy Qur'an:

(The other) said, "Verily you will not be able to have patience with me!" And how can you have patience about things of which your understanding is not complete?" (Surat al-Kahf, 18:67-68)

How you can be with company of *awliyaullah* when you cannot understand what they are doing? The ways of *awliyaullah* are completely different. When you reach the Maqām al-Wilayah, the Station of Sainthood, you have to get a clean and clear picture. If you get a fuzzy picture, it means your receiver is not good. To avoid that, you cannot listen to your ego because it will tell you, "The Shaykh said this but he meant that." Who gave you the authority to interpret that?

Sayyidina 'Abdul-Khāliq al-Ghujdawāni ق said, "O my son! I listened to you, but now it is my turn to ask you one very simple question. If you feel you can answer it, then truly you don't need a *murshid* and you may move forward by yourself. If you think you need me to answer and explain it to you, then you are obliged to have a *murshid*."

How to Destroy Black Magic

People are so lucky to find a real guide. Sayyidina 'Abdul Qadir al-Jilani ق said, "If you see someone flying in the air, know he is *Shaytan*, not a *wali*." There are false ones who use *jinn* to fly; they are possessed and they also use black magic to harm people. That is why too many questions are coming now on the Internet regarding black magic. Anyone using *jinn* for destruction is a fake one and when you say, "*a'ūdhu billāhi min ash-Shaytani 'r-rajīm*," their magic will fall down.

Grandshaykh ق narrated an account of Sayyidina Shaykh Sharafuddin ق that took place in 1913 in Aya Sofia, the big mosque in Istanbul, when he debated non-Muslim priests whom people had seen flying from the ground up to the balcony, rising up and coming down again and again. They had observed so much seclusion that Allah ﷻ gave them that power. The people were stunned and said, "These priests have truth if they are able to do that." People were confused by that, as such actions always bring *fitna*. So Shaykh Sharafuddin did something to stop their black magic, that was similar to what Shaykh 'Abdul-Khāliq al-Ghujdawāni ق answered his student.

Shah Naqshband ق said, "Our way is association and good is with the group."

To avoid showing the ego, *awliyaullah*, especially those from the high caliber of the Naqshbandi Golden Chain, have been ordered not to display their miraculous powers. Sometimes you might see something from them that is not considered miraculous power, but they are normal issues that they sprinkle around *murīds* to keep them united. The real miracle they perform is to work on your heart, to polish you and present you clean to the Prophet ﷺ every twenty-four hours!

Anyone who uses *jinn* in their lives are trying to cheat students, like in the time of Prophet ﷺ, when non-Muslim *jinn* entered the three idols the people worshipped—Hubal, al-Uzza and al-Lat—and they began to speak, which created *fitna*. Using *jinn* in that way is not accepted and that is why we have to be careful of so-called Shaykhs who are trying to destroy students of the real Masters by using *jinn* to make black magic.

Shaykh Sharafuddin ق entered Aya Sofia and turned his shoes upside down, showing the bottom side up and the top of the shoe down. As soon as he turned his shoes, the priests lost energy and fell down. Then Shaykh Sharafuddin ق put his shoes upside down at the mosque entrance, because what those priests were doing is *bātil*, so he displayed the backs of shoes, what touches dirt. Then he began to recite Surah YaSin in reverse, from its last letter to its first letter, and the black magic stopped.

Mawlana Shaykh Nazim is giving permission now for people who have been affected by *jinn* or black magic to overcome that. "Truth has come and falsehood has perished." So anyone who has a problem with black magic can recite Surah YaSin that way (in reverse), verse by verse, and continue until the black magic stops. If you stop reciting and the ill effects are not completely gone, recite up to seven verses, as we are not Shaykh Sharafuddin ق to recite it by heart backwards. Look at the ability of *awliyaullah*! When he reversed the recitation, immediately their magic finished!

`Abdul-Khaliq's Question that Ended the Debate

'Ubaydullah al-Amawi ق wondered, what is that question Sayyidina 'Abdul-Khāliq al-Ghujdawāni ق will ask? He was unable to sleep, thinking, "I know all these knowledges from the top to all the way down, so what more is there?" He could not resolve this because he had acquired all his knowledge in *dunya*, and Shaykh 'Abdul-Khāliq al-Ghujdawāni ق told him anything you acquire without a connection from *Ākhirah* will never stand on a firm structure, like building your house on a cliff:

أَفَمَنْ أَسَّسَ بُنْيَانَهُ عَلَى تَقْوَى مِنَ اللهِ وَرِضْوَانٍ خَيْرٌ أَمْ مَّنْ أَسَّسَ بُنْيَانَهُ عَلَىٰ شَفَا جُرُفٍ هَارٍ فَانْهَارَ بِهِ فِي نَارِ جَهَنَّمَ وَاللَّهُ لاَ يَهْدِي الْقَوْمَ الظَّالِمِينَ

Which then is best? He that lays his foundation on piety to Allah and His good pleasure, or He that lays his foundation on an undermined sand-cliff ready to crumble to pieces, and it does crumble to pieces with him, into the fire of Hell. And Allah guides not people that do wrong. (Surat at-Tawbah, 9:109)

That is why he pulled all the knowledge of Ahmad al-Badawi ق, as it was all built in *dunya*; only then was Shaykh 'Abdul-Khāliq able to pour heavenly knowledge into his heart.

Sayyidina 'Abdul-Khāliq al-Ghujdawāni ق asked 'Ubaydullah al-Amawi ق, "Do you remember a moment or a day in your other life when you were not a form in a subtle being, but a soul?"

Life does not begin when you are born. This *dunya* is a second life cycle, but real life, the first life cycle is in heavens when Allah ﷻ created you as a soul. The third life cycle is *barzakh*, from the grave up to Judgment Day, and from Judgment Day to Eternal Life is the fourth life cycle. It means, "Your *dunya* cycle is not important to me. Do you remember the pre-*dunya* life cycle?" 'Ubaydullah had no answer.

Then the Shaykh asked, "Do you remember the moment when Allah ﷻ asked you, 'Am I not your Lord?' and everyone answered 'Yes!'"

'Ubaydullah said, "No."

Sayyidina 'Abdul-Khāliq ق said, "Then whatever you have now is nothing. Most important is that moment and remembering it will give you the keys for your door. Do you remember that big Heavenly Day, and who was on your right side and on your left side all the way to the end, and their names in Heaven and in *dunya*? The souls are gathered troops all together; you must know them and *id`ūhum li-ābāhim*, 'Call them to their fathers (33:5).' Do you know their fathers?"

What can he answer? 'Ubaydullah said, "No."

Then Sayyidina 'Abdul-Khāliq al-Ghujdawāni ق said, "Everything you mentioned, the many high-level questions and high visions, are like a toddler trying to walk and falling down. You are nothing, and everything you told me is like toys and candies that *awliya* give their followers to keep them attracted to the Way."

So where are we? We wear big turbans, some walk with big sticks to make it appear they have some special knowledge. When all of them go to Mawlana Shaykh, he asks them, "What is your name?" as if to say, "You are nothing, so don't come here with pride!"

Shaykh 'Abdul-Khāliq ق said, "O my son! You have to take your *tarīqah* from a perfect Shaykh that can take you all the way: to know what you promised, what you received, what you are obliged to fulfill, and the help you will give those that listen to you. You will never reach that level without following a perfect Shaykh who can take you to that Day!"

Awliyaullah have that secret and they are waiting to give it to you, but you have to run for it, without waiting for everything to come to you. You have to do something that makes the Shaykh happy with you, and even then he will not give it easily; he will give too many tests until he crushes you.

"O my son! If you worshipped with the total worship of all *jinn* and *ins* from the time of Adam to Judgment Day and all kinds of openings come to you, it has no value, *lā 'itibara laha,* is not even considered and is thrown in your face, if you don't know what happened to you on the Day of Promises! Do you know what happened to me and to all *awliya* before me, in order to know all the knowledges of the Day of Promises? I will take you all the way there, but you have to drop all your visions from your hearts and whatever knowledges were unveiled to you. Don't look at it; throw them from your heart, because if you look at it I will not be able to take you to Day of Promises."

Today if someone sees a dream, he says, "O, I saw angels! I saw turbans! I went to Madinah and to Mecca!" Keep it to yourself; why talk about it? Because he feels from the ego side, "I saw that and it means I am going to be a *wali*." Dreams can open temptation and they send it to test if you will continue to fight your ego, or not. You must acknowledge, "This is from my Shaykh's love and favor, but I don't love him as much as he loves me." But these days, if someone sees anything even slightly good in a dream, suddenly he thinks he is a big Shaykh. Some people like that takes drugs and hallucinate, and they believe what they see, although it is false.

So Sayyidina 'Abdul-Khāliq al-Ghujdawāni ق is warning 'Ubaydullah al-Amawi ق, "I cannot give you even a drop of knowledge in this *tarīqah*, this journey of yours, except on one condition, which is necessary for you to understand and to carry the responsibility and this burden. If you continue to believe you are special, I cannot open to you, but if you surrender and throw everything from your heart and submit yourself in total humility, I can take you there."

Sayyidina Shaykh Sharafuddin said, "We don't want the submission of a dead person. Be like a leaf in the wind, with no will."

But Sayyidina 'Abdul-Khāliq ق even lowered the standard and said, "I can take you as a dead person in the hands of the washer. So if you accept, I can open for you, but if you don't accept, there is no permission to open anything!

Finally, 'Ubaydullah said, *"Ya Sayyidi,* I accept!"

The First Steps of Submission

Shaykh 'Abdul-Khāliq ق said, "First, you have to die. I am going to crush you. Are you ready to be destroyed? If you now devote your life to me, I will destroy your ego and take you all the way there in three hours. First I will wash you with what they washed me and you will begin to understand the knowledges you reached on Day of Promises. Prepare yourself!"

The spiritual vision of *awliyaullah* is not for their enjoyment, as to see angels, *jinn,* dreams and visions is child's play. *Tarīqah* is given based on two issues: 1) when you get it, it is your burden that you alone are responsible to carry, and 2) how will you uplift those listening to you. They don't give to you for your own pleasure, but rather to benefit those whom you will guide. So, to be a *wali* is not an easy task. People run after the fame and pretend to be Shaykhs for people to follow them, but where are they taking their followers?

A *wali* does not seek the spotlight as he works in anonymity. We saw this from Grandshaykh `AbdAllah who emerged from his one-year seclusion in 1967 and told us the Prophet ﷺ said to him, *"Ya waladī*! Don't go after people as I will send you the best of the *ummah,* sincere servants to whom you may deliver a message. Seclude yourself." *Awliyaullah* are responsible to deliver a message, and when they have gone so far in carrying that message and the burdens of people, Allah grants them rest as they have proven themselves. They are *al-kummal,* the perfect ones, the high-caliber Shaykhs of the Naqshbandi Golden Chain who completed their requirements and reached that high rank.

Mawlana Shaykh Nazim ق is in a similar situation now. He used to travel from one place to another, right and left, east and west, north and south. Now Prophet ﷺ said, "I am sending them to you." Before, Mawlana said, "I am going to their countries," but now he says, "If you want to come, come." Going from people to people is not easy, as there is too much negativity from one place to another, so whoever comes now are sincere ones whom, when they enter, will be cleaned.

Grandshaykh ق narrated how Shaykh Sharafuddin held a weekly, invitation-only *suhbah* reserved for specific followers that sat in assigned places, and all had to know their place and could not jump over others to get in.

In *fiqh*, in congregational prayers the only one eligible to pray directly behind the *imam* must be able to lead the prayer with all its requirements. Then if the *imam* loses *wudū* or for some reason can no longer lead the prayer, he steps back into the first rank and that one steps forward and leads the prayer. Alternately, the person to the right and to the left can step forward to lead the prayer, and those three places in the first rank are reserved for them. If the *imam* loses *wudū* during prayer, the prayer is not void, but the one behind the *imam* has to take his place.

Similarly, when disciples sit in the presence of the Shaykh they must know their places, and the reserved places to his right and left are designated for whom he appoints. *Tarīqah* is discipline; only children sit here and there.

Shaykh Sharafuddin saw someone uninvited approaching that private association to ask about a *dunya* issue and knew it would interrupt the *murīds'* attention. So he told his helper to go get an ornamented *jubbah* from the house, a gift from Sultan Abdul Hameed ؏ that was made of silk and lavishly embroidered with gold and silver thread and, therefore, Shaykh Sharafuddin had never worn it. As soon as that helper brought the jubbah, that man arrived.

Shaykh Sharafuddin ق said, "O! I was waiting for you as I have that *jubbah* for you; take it and go."

So they don't care what they have, they give and they don't want to disturb the association or the love directed to the Shaykh. Sometimes the Shaykh might ask, "Do you need anything?" and some answer "yes," while others answer "no." Grandshaykh ق taught us, if the Shaykh asks if you need anything, it is best to ask for his *du'a*.

So Shaykh 'Abdul-Khāliq al-Ghujdawāni ق told 'Ubaydullah al-Amawi ق, "In order to carry that you need a specialty, then I will give you all that."

'Ubaydullah said, "O my Shaykh, I am ready!"

Awliyaullah know we cannot reach levels the grandshaykhs reached, which is why they sit for two or three hours giving us guidance. That is why the *suhbah* is important. Shah Naqshband ق said, *Tariqatun as-suhbah wa 'l-*

khayru fi 'l-jami'yya. "Our way is association and the best way is sitting with the group."

Today they teach dirty things on Internet through Facebook and other websites that appear to be for entertainment and staying in contact with people, but it is really to know what everyone is doing and with whom they have a relationship. Young people are exposing themselves to bad, *Shaytanic* ones. Friends are your companions who, when you are hungry they are hungry, when you have food they have food, and when you are wealthy they are wealthy. The holy Companions of the Prophet ﷺ would do anything for you out of love. You have to have companionship with people who are dedicated to each other and who look after and help each other. You reach that by association with the Shaykh as it raises you up.

To not expose their knowledge, *awliyaullah* always keep a low profile and they don't speak about what you will have tomorrow or in which country you will end up or whether you will have children or not, as Allah said in Holy Qur'an, "*Allah will erase or confirm whatever He likes and with Him is the Mother of Books* (13:39)." So if a *wali* speaks on the future and he is not of the caliber that he can see what is confirmed or what will be erased, whatever he says might not be real, as Allah may change it if He wants. That is why it is *harām* when expectant parents do an ultrasound to find out if they will have a boy or girl. Allah ﷻ doesn't like that.

How many Shaykhs, *walīs*, speak of the coming of Mahdi ؏? Only one, and before him was another one, and before him another one. That shows us they completed their perfection and were issued a statement from Prophet ﷺ, "You have achieved that level and are authorized to speak of the Unseen future." That is why Mawlana Shaykh speaks about Sayyidina al-Mahdi ؏, and before him Grandshaykh, and before him Shaykh Sharafuddin, and before him Shaykh Abu Muhammad al-Madani, and before him Shaykh Abu Ahmad as-Sughuri, and before him Shaykh Jamaluddin al-Ghumuqi al-Husayni, and before him Shaykh Muhammad Effendi al-Yaraghi, and before him Shaykh Khas Muhammad, and before him Shaykh Ismail Muhammad ash-Shirwāni, back to Shaykh Khalid al-Baghdadi, may Allah ﷻ preserve their secrets! To achieve that perfection is not simple.

That is why the *kummal*, perfect ones, always like to speak in a common way instead of giving theories, because they are preparing their students to be in the presence of Prophet ﷺ and *awliyaullah*. That is the work of those who give theories and does not confirm a reality. Who presents theories is not confirming a reality, so he doesn't know the reality or reach it, and his argument may or may not be correct. So these days, most who think they are speaking from the connection of their hearts are not connected to a *wali*; they are connected to their ego and mislead whoever listens to them!

Sayyidina 'Abdul-Khāliq al-Ghujdawāni ق said, "*Ya waladī!* First of all, to show you what you promised Allah on the Day of Promises and what happened there, you have to attend my *suhbat* just like other disciples. Also, they are not at your level so you have to come down to their level and see yourself as if you are at the same level or less. All your visions don't mean anything to me and if you cling to them, in one moment you will be thrown out! Sayyidina Adam ﷺ turned his ear to another for one moment, so Allah ﷻ took him out of Paradise and revoked his heavenly visions. O my son! Just one mistake of your ego might take you out of all that heavenly knowledge.

"Our way is association, to sit with the *wali* and receive blessings reflecting on him from heavens, and to disseminate to the others sitting there. You must sit in association to clean and improve yourself, or you will not receive heavenly blessings or your Reality on Day of Promises. There you were in the company of Prophet ﷺ and in *dunya* you are not in his company, so to even be considered you need to spend time with and accompany a *wali* that inherits from Prophet ﷺ and then these blessings will come on you and day-by-day you will become perfect. That does not happen from your ego dressing you; rather, I take blessings from Prophet ﷺ and dress them on you! Therefore, whatever comes from your ego is considered useless and whatever you receive from *awliyaullah* is considered good."

'Ubaydullah said, "O my teacher, what must I do?"

Shaykh 'Abdul-Khāliq said, "You must be generous."

"What do you mean?"

"Whatever you have of *dunya* wealth and *Ākhirah* wealth, you must give to me (similar to Ahmad al-Badawi's story), because, "Whoever built his building on a cliff without strong infrastructure will fall down in Hellfire."[8] So whatever you built with your ego, you must be generous and

---

[8] Surat at-Tawbah, 9:109.

give it all for if you withhold it, you cannot take what I want to give you, which in three hours will take you to your reality that is embedded in the reality of Sayyidina Muhammad ﷺ! That reality, your atom, is dressed with the Light of Prophet ﷺ, just as everyone's real essence is embedded in Prophet's essence: "Know that the Messenger of Allah is in you (49:7)."

As written in Grandshaykh ق notes, Sayyidina 'Abdul-Khāliq continues, "If he is not within you, you cannot exist." Allah made every person appear because of the existence of Sayyidina Muhammad ﷺ in the Divine Presence; otherwise, you cannot appear, which means you are not created. You being here means you are created and in reality of Prophet ﷺ in the Divine Presence. That is why Prophet is always happy when Allah calls him "'abdī, My servant!" Until you understand this, you can never see your reality because first you must understand that you have no existence, you only exist through the existence of Prophet ﷺ! Therefore, you must surrender or you are nothing."

'Ubaydullah asked, "How do I surrender?"

Sayyidina 'Abdul-Khāliq ق answered, "If you take a drop from a cup of water with your fingertip, you see a drop has formed, but when it goes back into the cup of water it has no form, it goes back to an ocean. You must denounce your form and swim in the ocean of Prophet ﷺ. That is the key for you."

"How can I do that?" 'Ubaydullah asked.

Sayyidina 'Abdul-Khāliq ق said, "To do that is to be in the Shaykh's association, surrendering and submitting completely to his orders, your heart must be empty. You have to come with nothing, like a leaf in the wind goes wherever the wind throws it—right or left, up on the mountain, deep down into the valley—and then it is gone. Bring your self down. O my son, you must enter the demolition room."

The Demolition Room

Some people are cremated when they die, rendering their body to ashes, which is completely against Islamic *Shari`ah*. However, many mystics have spoken of crushing the disciple into powder or dust, after which the disciple might be dressed and then appear another time to speak to people.

To achieve that crushed state, in the language of *awliyaullah*, that is called "*Qahhār Tajāllī*, the Manifestation of The Subduer," The One that demolishes or overpowers everything. *Awliyaullah* like the process of annihilation from which your ego is completely destroyed. After that, you can never raise your head and say, "*Labbayk*, I am here," because in their language the word "I" is absent; they use the plural "we," not the singular. Then they will not be asked; they will be excused. To say "I" is to speak about yourself. "We" means all of us are the same.

Sayyidina 'Abdul-Khāliq ق said, "You must go into that demolition room for Allah's Beautiful Name, *al-Qahhār*, to shatter you into dust and completely annihilate you. Then I will take you to the level of *baqa`*, "complete existence," where you will exist in the presence of Prophet ﷺ and there will be no more 'you' and 'me'. Like the drop of water disappears in the cup, you will disappear in the presence of the Prophet ﷺ. When you reach that level, through *awliyaullah*, Prophet ﷺ will open to you to know the Day of Promises and the *awrād* that was written for you and how to act accordingly.

Sayyidina 'Abdul-Khāliq ق continued, "O my son! I must tell you about Shah Naqshband ق.[9] After all that, Shah Naqshband will appear in *dunya*, but he will never give his followers what I am giving you because he will not accept to speak. Shah Naqshband entered the demolition room not once, but fifty-one times! He goes in, comes out and then goes back in to be sure he is completely annihilated and that no trace of ego remains on him, and he will annihilate himself in the presence of Allah ﷻ, the Prophet ﷺ and *awliyaullah* ق. His *dharrah* (atom) will be able to speak there, but before he reaches that level he will not speak in *dunya*. Then whatever he is able to get, his words will come directly from the reality of the Existence and the Creation of Sayyidina Muhammad ﷺ!"

Sayyidina 'Abdul-Khāliq ق continued, "Be happy that we accept you to go into the demolition room once! In our time once is enough, but in the future they cannot accept you unless you go fifty-one times like Sayyidina Shah Naqshband ق. *Man tashabbaha bi-qawmin fa huwa minhu.* 'Who imitates or follows a group of people, that saint will be with them.' Sayyidina Shah Naqshband ق did not accept less than fifty-one times for himself and for his *murīds*, so it's going to be tough. That's why you see now no one is able to reach that except for few *awliyaullah*. That's why we call them *Sultan ul-*

---

[9] Shah Naqshband came after 'Abdul Khāliq al-Ghujdawāni. 'Abdul Khāliq has authority to speak about the future because he is one of the *kummal*.

Awliya, because they went into a process of being demolished fifty-one times; they were crushed over and over and over again. Then Allah ﷻ sends them back, from the Ocean of Annihilation to the Ocean of Existence. At that time I will take you to your trust, to know who is on your right, who is on your left, what you promised, and how to achieve it."

'Ubaydullah al-Amawi ق said, "O my Shaykh! I am ready, and I give all my wealth and all my knowledge."

۞ ... ۩

In three hours, Sayyidina 'Abdul-Khāliq ق pulled out all his knowledge and made him zero or less, and threw him into the demolition room and was able to perfect him into his reality of Existence on the Day of *Alastu bi-Rabbikum,* and he was able to go there! So we are asking through our *shuyukh* ق and through Prophet ﷺ, "We are weak servants and we cannot do that by ourselves without looking at our shortcomings. *Ya Rabbī!* We are helpless and hopeless. Open from Your Generosity Oceans without looking at our shortcomings, and dress us with the reality of the Day of *Alastu bi-Rabbikum!*"

Allah ﷻ tests His servants and some of them became like thunder, never doubting and never questioning. I spoke with one of them yesterday; he knows himself and that Allah gave him such reality in his heart that his openness and generosity defies description. He never had any doubt in his heart, and immediately, without delay, says "Yes!" for everything. May Allah give that person from His Endless Oceans *dunya* wealth and *Ākhirah* wealth. And may Allah keep us all under the wings or arms of Sayyidi Shaykh Muhammad Nazim al-Haqqani, *Sultan al-Awliya,* and keep us all together!

With this, we end the excellent story of 'Ubaydullah al-Amawi ق with Shaykh 'Abdul Khāliq al-Ghujdawāni ق. May Allah ﷻ preserve their secrets!

May Allah ﷻ forgive us and may Allah ﷻ bless us.

Wa min Allahi 't-tawfiq, bi hurmati 'l-habīb, bi hurmati 'l-Fatihah.

And with Allah is success. For the sake of the Beloved, for his sake we recite the opening chapter of Holy Qur'an.

The Sajda Under the Throne of Allah

*A'ūdhu billāhi min ash-Shaytani 'r-rajīm. Bismillāhi' r-Raḥmāni 'r-Raḥīm.
Nawaytu 'l-arbā'īn, nawaytu 'l-'itikāf, nawaytu'l-khalwah, nawaytu 'l-'uzlah,
nawaytu 'r-riyaḍa, nawaytu 's-sulūk, lillāhi Ta'alā fī hādhā 'l-masjid.
Ati'ūllāha wa ati'ū 'r-Rasūla wa ūli 'l-amri minkum.
Obey Allah, obey the Prophet, and obey those in authority among you. (4:59)*

We mentioned that 'Ubaydullah al-Amawi ق described all kinds of knowledges he possessed, including knowledge of the *sajda* of the believers, because when they sleep their soul makes *sajda* under the Heavenly Throne.

From the secret of that *sajda*, Allah ﷻ gave visions for *awliyaullah* to use the power of that *sajda* to take their students to reach the presence of Sayyidina Muhammad ﷺ once every 24 hours. From the secret of that *sajda* came *Salat an-Najāt* and we perform the long *sajda* after praying the two *raka'ats*. That is to open oceans of knowledges that are under *al-'Arsh*, and there is no description for that heavenly creature that Allah ﷻ created.

> *Taha. We have not sent down the Qur'an to you to be (an occasion) for your distress, but only as an admonition to those who fear (Allah), a revelation from Him Who created the earth and the heavens on high. (Allah) Most Gracious is firmly established on the Throne (of authority). (Surah TaHa, 20:1-5)*

One *Ahlu 's-Sunnah wa 'l-Jama'ah* beliefs that differs from other ideologies is that Allah doesn't need a throne to sit on, because, "He overtook the Throne." It is said that when Allah ﷻ created the Throne, He created nineteen angels to carry it as Allah wants to show His power to angels in Heaven, so these huge, indescribable angels lifted the Throne and were happy to carry it, and all other angels looked at them, surprised at how much power Allah gave His angels to carry the Throne, as mentioned in Ayat al-Kursi:

> *Wasi'a kursiyyuhu 's-samāwāti wa 'l-arḍ wa lā ya'ūduhū hifzhuhuma wa Huwa 'l-'Aliyyi 'l-'Azhīm.*
>
> *His Throne extends over the heavens and the earth, and He feels no fatigue in guarding and preserving them, for He is the Most High, the Supreme (in Glory).* (Surat al-Baqara, 2:255)

The *Kursi* is not the Throne, *al-'Arsh*. 'Arsh is different and *Kursi* is different. Allah said the *Kursi*, *samāwāti wa 'l-ard*, is bigger than this universe and the heavens. The *'Arsh* overtook heavens and earth and then Allah overtook everyone. So those angels were so happy, carrying it, and then Allah ordered the *'Arsh* to carry them, and the angels were holding onto it, so as not to fall; they had no power to carry. When Allah wants to give power He gives, and when He orders the *'Arsh* to carry them to show His Will, only that is considered.

So *Ahlu 's-Sunnah wa 'l-Jama'at* believe that the boundaries of time and space do not apply to Allah and that He 'overtook' the Throne. A different ideology says Allah physically 'sits on the Chair,' which is anthropomorphism. *Salat an-Najāt* came from that, and when we make *sajda* in *Salat an-Najāt* we are making it under the Throne, where any *du'a* is accepted; if you don't get the answer of your *du'a* now then you will get it later, or at the time of death, or in your grave. That is why it is important to pray *Salat an-Najāt*.

So 'Ubaydullah al-Amawi ق was happy and proud to speak about that, saying, "*Ya Sayyidi!* I know what happened to me in that *sajda*. I received all those knowledges and am becoming oceans because of it. So does one with all these heavenly knowledges opened to his heart still need a *murshid*?" He thought he was a *murshid*, so why take another? That is sickness in the heart, and as we mentioned, the Prophet described the sign of a *munāfiq* as *'alīmun bi 'l-lisān, jahūlan bi 'l-qalb*, "very eloquent speakers but ignorant in the heart."

That often happens to those who study Islam from a teacher who is not Muslim, or from Muslim teachers who are not practicing, because know how to speak, they are eloquent, but they are ignorant in their hearts so they don't get the 'taste.' 'Ubaydullah al-Amawi ق was tasting, which is why he wanted to know the truth. He was in the level of inheriting from Sayyidina Musa, which is why he is called "Musawi," and that is why he inherited the character of asking too many questions in his quest for the truth. That is when Allah sent Sayyidina Musa to one of His servants and he was stunned, as mentioned in Holy Qur'an when Sayyidina Khidr asked Musa:

And how will you be patient about something you never saw or heard?

(Surat al-Kahf, 18:68)

This is why when we didn't hear something or see it, we don't accept it. If you accept you are submitting and Allah ﷻ will open, which is why *'Imān al-Ghayb*, Belief in the Unseen, is so important!

So that is why when the Prophet ﷺ asked the *Sahābah* ؓ, "Who is the best among all creation?" they answered, "The Prophets ؑ." He said, "How is it the Prophets when they see what they see, receive the messages they receive, and when Jibrīl comes to them?" It means yes, they are best in rank as Allah ﷻ honored them to be His Prophets, but belief in the Unseen is different. They said, "Then it is the angels," and Prophet ﷺ said, "When they see all that they see, how would they not accept?" They said, "*Ya Rasūlullah*, it is us, your Companions." He said, "When you see me you see the truth, so how would you not believe?" Then they said, "Who are these people?" Prophet ﷺ said, "The best among all the creation is they who come after me, but who will believe in me without seeing me. They are *ikhwani*, 'my brothers.'" It means he made them equal in blood and they have the 'blood secret.'

When 'Ubaydullah al-Amawi ق narrated all his knowledges, experiences, visions and accomplishments, essentially he was saying, "I am so powerful." Then after a time, Shaykh 'Abdul Khāliq al-Ghujdawāni ق told him, "Look at all these students who are better than you, because you see all that and still don't submit, and they are not seeing anything and they submit."

Someone with too much knowledge risks becoming arrogant, which is why many professors are prone to think they conquered the universe. Nimrod threw Sayyidina Ibrahim ؑ in the fire because he told Nimrod, "You are not my Lord!" Nimrod was shocked and said of all the statues they worshipped, the statue of him was the biggest, so how can you not worship me? That night Sayyidina Ibrahim ؑ secretly cut the statues' heads except the statue of Nimrod.

When the people saw all the heads cut, they went to Nimrod, crying, "O our master! This is what happened."

> *They said, "We heard a youth talk of them: he is called Abraham." They said, "Then bring him before the eyes of the people so they may bear witness." They said, "Are you the one that did this with our gods, O Abraham?" He said, "No, this was done by—this is their biggest one! Ask them, if they can speak intelligently!" So they turned to themselves and said, "Surely you are the ones in the wrong!"* (Surat al-Anbiya, 21: 60-64)

Nimrod said, "Who did that?"

Sayyidina Ibrahim ﷺ said, "You said yourself you are God, but you don't know who did that? Go and ask the biggest one, he'll give you the answer."

How to ask a statue? So the people knew they were wrong to worship statues, and Nimrod looked foolish and he wanted to take revenge on Sayyidina Ibrahim ﷺ, so he built a huge minaret to climb and shoot at the sky. Allah ﷻ caused a bird to be hit and the arrow was stained with blood. At that, Nimrod said, "Look! I killed the Lord of Ibrahim."

See how arrogance pollutes the heart and feeds unbelief! Today if you say "God," "Allah," or "*Dieu*" in French, people look at you with disgust, as if you are illiterate, because they reject faith.

May Allah ﷻ forgive us and may Allah ﷻ bless us.

Wa min Allahi 't-tawfiq, bi hurmati 'l-ḥabīb, bi hurmati 'l-Fatihah.

And with Allah is success. For the sake of the Beloved, for his sake we recite the opening chapter of Holy Qur'an.

Five Magnificent Favors Allah Grants in Ramadan

A'ūdhu billāhi min ash-Shaytani 'r-rajīm. Bismillāhi' r-Raḥmāni 'r-Raḥīm.
Nawaytu 'l-arbā'īn, nawaytu 'l-'itikāf, nawaytu'l-khalwah, nawaytu 'l-'uzlah,
nawaytu 'r-riyaḍa, nawaytu 's-sulūk, lillāhi Ta'alā fī hādhā 'l-masjid.
Ati'ūllāha wa ati'ū 'r-Rasūla wa ūli 'l-amri minkum.
Obey Allah, obey the Prophet, and obey those in authority among you. (4:59)

O Muslims! O Believers! In *Ramadan*, no one knows what or how much Allah ﷻ will reward His servants when they fast for Him. It is not like the reward of the prayers, because when you pray it is for you to demonstrate, "O Allah! You are my Lord and I am Your servant." Allah ﷻ gives us an explanation of the importance and divine favors of the sacred month of *Ramadan*, in which the Holy Qur'an was revealed to Sayyidina Muhammad ﷺ:

> *Ramadan is the (month) in which was sent down the Qur'an, as a guide to mankind, also clear (signs) for guidance and judgment (between right and wrong). So every one of you who is present (at his home) during that month should spend it in fasting, but if anyone is ill or on a journey, the prescribed period (should be made up) by days later. Allah intends every facility for you; He does not want to put you into difficulties. (He wants you) to complete the prescribed period, and to glorify Him in that He has guided you and so you shall be grateful.* (Surat al-Baqara, 2:185)

Allah ﷻ said to the Prophet ﷺ:

> *Fasting is for Me and I will reward those who fast not through my angels, but directly.*   Hadīth Qudsī

How dare you then, as a Muslim, not fast when Allah ﷻ is saying, "I will reward you directly!" Allah's Rewards are not like human rewards! When you stop eating, when you stop backbiting, when you stop every kind of bad thing, you think Allah ﷻ is not going to reward you for every *hasanāt*. He says, "Fasting is for Me and I will reward you directly!"

All those who are not fasting during *Ramadan*, shame on you here in this life and shame on you on the Day of Judgment! When Allah ﷻ says, "*Ramadan* is for Me! What did you do for Me?" can you say, "O Allah, I did not fast!" You will tremble there to remember you didn't fast *Ramadan* in *dunya*. And people might give many excuses, like some time ago when the president of a country in North Africa issued a *fatwa* that manual laborers don't have to fast and instead he gave them a vacation! We say, sell your resorts for millions of dollars, give it to them and let them fast the month of *Ramadan*!

Sayyidina Muhammad ﷺ said, "My *ummah* has been given five things in the month of *Ramadan* that no prophet before me was given." Look at Allah's Mercy on us!

The first favor is granted on the first night of *Ramadan*, as soon as the month started but you didn't fast yet. Then, Allah ﷻ looks at the whole Ummat an-Nabī ﷺ but not at who is fasting or not, but simply He ﷻ looks at all of them and showers upon them *Tajalliyat al-Jamal*, Manifestations of His Beauty!

It is very well known that whomever Allah ﷻ looks upon with the Divine Manifestation of His Beautiful Names and Attributes, He will never punish. If Allah is looking at someone with that Divine Look of Mercy and Beauty and *maghfirah* since the beginning of *Ramadan*, do you think Allah ﷻ will throw him into Hellfire? Allah is not like us: when He gives, He gives and He doesn't take it back, but when we give, we like to take it back. Allah will not punish him: He is Merciful. So we don't want to be ashamed when you break your fast for no reason.

Allah ﷻ said in Holy Qur'an:

(Fast) for a fixed number of days, but if any of you is ill or on a journey, the same number (should be made up) from other days. And as for those who can fast with difficulty, they have (a choice either to fast or) to feed a poor person (for every day). But whoever does good of his own accord, it is better for him. And that you fast, it is better for you if only you know.

(Surat al-Baqara, 2:184)

Allah ﷻ gives you an excuse, but know that you must fast. Still there are people not fasting, but still Allah looks at them that first night because they say, "*Lā ilāha illa-Llāh Muhammadur Rasulullah.*"

The second favor granted by Allah ﷻ is His pleasure from their fasting breath. People who are fasting wake up in the morning and brush their teeth, but Allah did not allow you to brush your teeth when you fast. Allah said to His Prophet ﷺ, "The smell of their breath when they fast is dearer to Me than the scent of musk." You are not putting anything in your mouth and your breath turns sour, but to Allah it is a heavenly smell; musk is the fragrance of heavens. So Allah is saying the breath of the one who fasts is more lovely than the fragrance of heavens, so don't worry that people will think you have bad breath because that smell is better than musk. Allah ﷻ changes it to a beautiful smell so the angels can approach you (they don't approach bad breath). That is one big reason not to smoke cigarettes; also, it is not accepted. Scholars say it is *makrūh* (undesirable), but *makrūh* repeated many times becomes something else. Cigarettes make you smell bad and your mouth dirty, so don't smoke!

Prophet ﷺ was praying *tarawīh* in *Ramadan* with the *Sahābah* ؇ and Sayyidina Jibrīl ؑ came with Divine Revelation, but he did not fully descend.

Prophet ﷺ said, "Jibrīl, why are you not coming down?" He said, "Some of your *Sahābah* ate onions and garlic, and from that smell I cannot come nearer." So Prophet ﷺ ordered those *Sahābah* to move away, but they loved Prophet ﷺ so they didn't move. Prophet ﷺ wanted the revelation to come, so he said, "'Umar, go smell their mouths," and as soon as they heard 'Umar coming they all ran away! Prophet ﷺ said, "I am going to send that same manifestation, *tajalli*, that is coming on us."

Angels will never take the prayers of smokers. That is why *Zakat al-Fitr* came, because there are a lot of mistakes in your fast and that payment compensates for them, so don't forget to pay your *Zakat al-Fitr* on time.

The third favor granted by Allah ﷻ is the angels ask for forgiveness from Allah ﷻ day and night on behalf of those who fast. So why are you making excuses to break your fast? In Arab countries, when *Ramadan* arrives some people travel far from home to be exempt from the fast, especially in summer. They want to cheat Allah ﷻ, as if He doesn't know their intentions!

Once I was on a plane coming from one very well-known Muslim country in the Middle East to London, a four-hour flight. A husband and wife sat with their family in business class. I was fasting. When food came, they ordered wine with it and the women removed their black *jilbabs* and ate and drank with their husbands, saying, "Because we are travelers." Prophet ﷺ traveled in the desert in dry weather, when one cannot breathe from the heat of the sun that 'bakes' you, and still they fasted!

The fourth favor granted by Allah is for those who are fasting in *dunya* when the time of their death arrives. Prophet said, "Decorate yourself." Allah instructs the angels, "Put ornaments all around because My servants are coming to My territory and they fasted for Me, so I will reward them to enter without any *hisāb* (account)."

The fifth favor granted by Allah in *Ramadan* is on the last night, when He forgives those who fasted and declares their innocence from the Hellfire.

ഌ ... ൦ള

The first ten days of *Ramadan* is full of Allah's Mercy; the second ten days is full of Allah's Forgiveness, and in the last ten days of *Ramadan*, Allah grants freedom from the Hellfire.

O Muslims! As we are granted such great rewards, we must always look forward to fasting in the holy month of *Ramadan* and not think it is too difficult!

May Allah forgive us and may Allah bless us.

Wa min Allahi 't-tawfīq, bi hurmati 'l-habīb, bi hurmati 'l-Fatihah.

And with Allah is success. For the sake of the Beloved, for his sake we recite the opening chapter of Holy Qur'an.

Prophet Foretold 360 Energy Points

*A'ūdhu billāhi min ash-Shaytani 'r-rajīm. Bismillāhi' r-Rahmāni 'r-Rahīm.
Nawaytu 'l-arbā'īn, nawaytu 'l-'itikāf, nawaytu'l-khalwah, nawaytu 'l-'uzlah,
nawaytu 'r-riyada, nawaytu 's-sulūk, lillāhi Ta'alā fī hādhā 'l-masjid.
Ati'ūllāha wa ati'ū 'r-Rasūla wa ūli 'l-amri minkum.
Obey Allah, obey the Prophet, and obey those in authority among you. (4:59)*

O Muslims! O Human Beings! Allah ﷻ sent Messengers and Prophets to guide humanity to what He likes because He wants humanity to be good so they will live in harmony.

He ﷻ said in the Holy Qur'an:

Fa alhamaha fujūraha wa taqwaha.
He inspired the self of its good and its bad.   (Surat ash-Shams, 91:8)

Just as the constellations orbit on a fixed time and keep the right distance from each other, they function the way Allah ﷻ wants and they never said, "No." Allah ﷻ said in Holy Qur'an:

Wa laqad karamna Bani Adam.
We have honored the Children of Adam.   (Surat al-'Isrā, 17:70)

He ﷻ wants us to understand what is good and He rewards us for whatever we do that is good.

The Prophet ﷺ related numerous authentic *ahadīth* narrated by the wife of the Prophet, Sayyida A'yesha ؓ. Look how Islam honored women, from whom we have learned what the Prophet ﷺ did or said! Sayyida A'yesha ؓ spread that knowledge and people up to today are doing what she told them, because after the Prophet ﷺ left this world she passed that knowledge with accuracy to the *Sahābah* ؓ.

Narrated by Sayyida A'yesha ؓ, the Prophet ﷺ said, "Allah ﷻ gave all human beings 360 pressure points." Sayyidina Muhammad ﷺ said this 1400 years ago. It was further revealed that any of the 360 points you press has an effect on the body. Also, very few have learned and practiced that knowledge. However, Prophet ﷺ said there is such knowledge, which reminds us of the famous *hadīth*:

Atlub al-'ilm wa law fi's-sīn.
Seek knowledge even in China. (Muslim)

Acupuncture, which also uses 360 or 366 pressure points, originated in China, and that beautiful *hadīth* shows us the Chinese were granted that talent.

Prophet ﷺ said, "There are 360 different *mafsal*, pressure points." If you physically press them, the body is relieved of pain and affliction. Accordingly, the soul also has 360 corresponding points that need to be checked and used, so just as we accept a physical guide to perform acupuncture on these points, we must accept a spiritual guide to move or put pressure on the spiritual pressure points.

The Prophet ﷺ gave you a very simple equation to derive spiritual benefit from these pressure points. We go to doctors who put their needles or press these points as the treatment and the problem still returns, but when you treat the spiritual pressure points you relieve that problem in a way that you won't need acupuncture treatment for that again. So the Prophet ﷺ said, use what he ﷺ said to activate the 360 points and when evening comes you will be removed from Hellfire, which means removed from difficulties in *dunya* and *Ākhirah*.

Supplications that Replace Badness with Goodness

Also, these 360 points are very important in removing anger, malice, hatred, envy and aggression; they can take all these away. When you become a subtle person, you will be happy and will find your illnesses resolved and you render it to Allah ﷻ. You are not worrying too much anymore as you are submitting to Allah ﷻ.

For example, yesterday we saw a young child sitting in a chair eating and she somehow fell, and no one knows how her *tawīz* caught on the chair and suspended her! That happened because of her purity and innocence, and Allah ﷻ saved her like when He ﷻ commanded:

"O Fire! Be thou cool and peaceful on Ibrahim!" (Surat al-Anbiya, 21:69)

Even if you are in fire, when Allah ﷻ wants you to feel a cool breeze you will feel it by following the way of Prophet ﷺ! So from the *barakah* of *Ramadan* and that *iftār*, nothing happened to that child. When we follow what Prophet ﷺ taught us, difficulties leave us.

Abu Hurayrah ؓ narrated from the Prophet ﷺ:

Man kabbar Allah wa hamadAllah wa halala lillāhi wa sabahAllah wa'staghfarahu wa 'azal hajar 'ani 't-tarīq.

Whoever magnified Allah and praised Allah and recited the tahlīl (Lā ilāha illa-Llāh) and glorified Allah and sought Allah's forgiveness and removed a stone from the way." Bukhari and Muslim

"To remove a stone from the way," means to help others, remove obstacles in their path, and also includes calling them to goodness, or in the case of someone doing something bad, if you know them you might advise them against it. It means whoever makes *tahlīl* and *SubhanAllah* and *istaghfirūllāh* and *tawbah*, so say, "O Allah! You are the Greatest, You are Lord of heavens and earth! Thank You for creating us and we must worship You and thank You and glorify You, and we must make *istighfār* for You." When you do that daily 360 times by saying, *"Allahu Akbar, alhamdulillah, labbayk Allahumma labbayk, subhanAllah, astaghfirullah,"* each 72 times, it totals 360, by Maghrib that day punishment will be removed from anything bad you did and Hellfire will not be written for you and you will be taken to Paradise!

There are many punishments in *dunya*, so complete this supplication daily to avoid difficulties. That is why people often recite so many *tasabīh* of the Prophet ﷺ. If you recite one time, *"HasbunAllah wa ni'mal-wakīl"* and *"SubhanAllah wa bi-hamdihi SubhanAllah al-'Azhīm, istaghfirullah,"* Allah ﷻ will give you a house in Paradise!

Prophet ﷺ said, "Whoever goes to the *masjid* (however you came, walking or by car) in the evening and in the morning, Allah ﷻ will give him a *nuzul*, a new place to settle whenever he goes and comes." That means in Allah's heavenly day and night He will grant you a better and higher place than the one He gave previously—we can say a palace or castle—in Heaven, *"qasrah fi 'l- Jannah."*

May Allah ﷻ open His Heavens for us and keep us in the company of Prophet ﷺ, *ma' alladhīna ana'ma Allahu 'alayhim min an-nabiyīn wa 's-ṣiddiqīn wa 'sh-shuhadā'i wa 's-sālihīn wa hasuna ulā'ika rafīqah.*

May Allah ﷻ forgive us and may Allah ﷻ bless us.

Wa min Allahi 't-tawfīq, bi hurmati 'l-habīb, bi hurmati 'l-Fatihah.
And with Allah is success. For the sake of the Beloved, for his sake we recite the opening chapter of Holy Qur'an.

The Adab of Eating

A'ūdhu billāhi min ash-Shaytani 'r-rajīm. Bismillāhi' r-Raḥmāni 'r-Raḥīm.
Nawaytu 'l-arbā'īn, nawaytu 'l-'itikāf, nawaytu'l-khalwah, nawaytu 'l-'uzlah,
nawaytu 'r-riyaḍa, nawaytu 's-sulūk, lillāhi Ta'alā fī hādhā 'l-masjid.
Ati'ūllāha wa ati'ū 'r-Rasūla wa ūli 'l-amri minkum.
Obey Allah, obey the Prophet, and obey those in authority among you. (4:59)

As we said before, "*Tarīqah* is built on good manners." *Tarīqah* is the essence of Islam within the framework of Islamic behaviors. This means if we don't have good manners, it is as if someone is outside of what Prophet ﷺ brought. As you like to dress and speak nicely, these actions have their own discipline and respect.

You cannot cross the limits. When you have a red light you cannot pass, you have to stop. When you have a green light you can move. So in Islam you must know the red light before you know the green light, because if you don't know where to stop, you might make lots of mistakes. The red light is important so you can stop desires and selfishness, or else you could go beyond limits and fall down any moment.

Everything we do has specific characteristics or protocols to remember Allah ﷻ. And I would like to address this issue that everyone needs every day and no one can live without. People might wonder what is that thing you cannot live without? It is important to know. If we think little bit, we have the answer. What is that? (One *murīd* said "food," one said "water," one said "air.") The first answer was right. You cannot live without food, which is the main need, then the others will come. Even in hospital you need food.

When you go to work, you dress nicely so people can see you as handsome or beautiful. Also, when you eat you have to give the highest respect in front of the food. People today eat with hungry eyes, as if they never saw food and that is *shirk*. Prophet ﷺ most often ate most barley bread that was hard and had stones in it; he ate it with water, salt and vinegar or oil. *Alhamdulillah*, that was a complete meal for Prophet ﷺ!

Today you are fasting. If they bring you bread, oil and vinegar, you will get angry and go to a restaurant; you won't say *"alhamdulillah"* if there is only vinegar, oil and bread. There are people in Pakistan and Africa who have no food! Allah ﷻ provides us the best food and still we complain it is not good or not enough or what we want.

In 1960 in Mawlana Shaykh Nazim's ق house in Damascus, it was his habit that when people went to sleep, he went to the kitchen to a closed cabinet with a wire screen with small holes for air, opened it and checked on food that is spoiled. He put it aside for the next day, the smelliest food, and while he offered his guests the good food, he ate the spoiled food, sometimes with mold and spots, not giving it to anyone else. Today, will you do that? No one will do that. Tons of food will be thrown away. Islam came to teach us how to eat!

In diplomatic protocol trainings, they teach you the protocols of eating with manners. They give lessons that Iblīs likes! You go to a restaurant and see most people eat with their left hand, with the fork in their left hand and knife in the right hand, because *Shaytan* whispered in their ears. Prophet ﷺ said if anyone eats with his left hand, he has no right. I am seeing many people downstairs eating and drinking with their left hand. There is no *barakah* in that; even worse, it becomes a sickness for you.

Take Each Bite with "Bismillah"

So, Islam came with a very high respect and discipline in the way to eat. Prophet ﷺ said in the beginning, when you want to eat, begin with *"Bismillah."* Imam Ghazali ؓ explained, "When you begin eating, say *'Bismillah'* in a loud voice," that is meant to remind the one beside you to say it as well. He will get the *barakah* of both, and it will become like a chain that protects *Shaytan* from entering your food. It is advisable to say *"Bismillah"* on every bite. Do we say it? Might be some do, especially when you have curry in front of you!

Imam Ghazali ؓ said, "If you say *'Bismillah'* on every bite, it is good and better, because it delays you from being too greedy as you are eating with *adab* and patience." Some people have no time to say *"Bismillah"* because they eat so quickly and their eyes are so hungry (with greed) and they look all over the table to see if others are eating better than them. So saying *"Bismillah"* delays you, and you must not eat quickly. That is why when you visit *awliyaullah,* the food takes one hour to finish. Today, people eat much too quickly!

When you make *dhikr* on that food, how can it harm you? Prophet ﷺ said, "The stomach is the house of illness." So when you remember to say "*Bismillah,*" you are eating with *dhikr* and it becomes *barakah* and cures you, because health is a combination of *dhikrullah* and food.

And Prophet said, "One has to eat with the right hand and begin and end with salt." Many people are doing that, especially Mawlana's *murīds*.

And Prophet said, "One has to make the bite very small." Not putting a big spoonful in your mouth, but a smaller spoonful. Some people are shoveling more and more in their mouths, one huge bite after another, not leaving food for others! So what you need to do?

Prophet said, "One has to chew very well and not swallow quickly." Do you notice when Mawlana Shaykh eats, a bite of bread is enough for a bird. I am surprised that he takes the piece of bread smaller than one-third length of your finger, eating so slowly, chewing very well. Prophet ﷺ ordered us to make the bite as small as you can, because during the time you are sitting at the table angels are descending, because when you begin with *"Bismillah"* and salt, those angels come, more and more, and their *tasbih* is written for you!

The Harm of Hungry Eyes

Don't have hungry eyes! I noticed many people, when you put food on the table and you cannot reach the end, your eyes always go there, and you ask people to pass you that one. Eat from in front of you! There is soup in front of you, or meat, say *alhamdulillah*. Don't be greedy. You have no right to put the bite in your mouth, swallow quickly, and quickly put your hand to take the next bite even before you swallow what is in your mouth! This is the *sunnah* of Prophet. In his time people ate from the same plate, to make sure everyone has a chance to eat (not piling food on individual plates, as we do today). Today people are shoveling in their mouth, and others have none. People search for the meat in rice dishes, and leave the rice behind!

You have no right to extend your hand until the first bite is swallowed. Be patient. Even if whole food is finished, let yourself be hungry for the love of your brothers. I see many people want to be served first and are not happy. Many take their time (on the serving line in the *dargah* dining hall) and choose their foods so carefully, examining each dish, and they move so slowly, moving the food around to inspect it, wondering should they take from this or that. Watch them and see how long they take; you will stay like that for hours! And I see many people, they are good ones, who will take any leftover food; they are happy with that. Don't be greedy. Give your brother priority over your selfishness. This is Islam: do not give priority to yourself!

And never say something bad about food. If it has salt or not enough salt, taste or no taste, never say anything bad about food, because it is Allah's Ni'mah (benevolence). People object. I know many husbands complain about their wives cooking, which is not good because it removes *barakah* from the food.

Prophet said, "Eat whatever is within one's reach, not what cannot be reached." Accept that Allah ﷻ gave it to that one and not you. That's why it's better to sit at a round table because you can reach everything on it! But when you sit on the floor to eat and you cannot reach all the food, why are you asking? Wait until the other person thinks about you and passes it along. Most people today are not like that; they finish the meat and say, "Now it's your turn," and only the bones are left! These are sticky issues with everyone.

So Prophet ﷺ extended his hand to only what was near him, except you can extend your hand to the fruit. The *Sahābah* ؓ asked, "Why only fruits, Ya Rasūlullah?" At that time they often had only one dish, with rice on one side and meat on the other side.

About eating fruits, Prophet ﷺ said, "It is different kinds of fruits, so you have the right to ask and take."

He ﷺ also said, "You have no right to eat from the middle of the tray. You eat from the circumference of the tray nearest you."

In Prophet's time, if a bite of food fell on the straw mat or floor, they cleaned it off and ate it. Today they throw away not only what drops but what is on their plate, as well. Why did you put so much food on the plate, why not a little? Because your eyes are hungry. Eyes are never full. Stomachs may be full. Some people also eat and then intentionally vomit (purge). If you throw food away, you are leaving it for *Shaytan*.

Today, we are leaving it, and it might be the *barakah* of that meal was in the last bite! That is why Prophet ﷺ said, "Don't clean your hand with the towel; lick your fingers because the *barakah* is there." It is *sunnah* to wash your hands before eating, because you lick your fingers after eating. Who is doing that now? We don't know where the *barakah* of that food is; it may be in the first bite.

Bread Is from Heavens, So Honor It!

He ﷺ also said, "You must eat food with bread and never cut bread with a knife." Cutting with a knife is reserved for meat and vegetables, as bread is a heavenly provision so use your hand to tear it. Today, everyone cuts bread with a knife, which is from *Shaytan*. Then they usually had dry bread and Prophet ﷺ used his hand to break it slowly.

Prophet ﷺ said, "Honor the bread. Allah ﷻ sent it down from the *barakah* of heavens." Today, no one honors the bread. No one touches it until you force them. Hajjah Naziha is upset about this. Take, take, take bread for the *barakah* and to honor that food! Bread and rice are the most blessed foods. Your stomach will be full if you eat the bread with vegetables and meat, but not without eating the bread. Mawlana Shaykh ق eats soup daily, but not before he breaks bread into pieces and puts it in the soup (a *sunnah* of Prophet). Honor the bread! Prophet used dip the dry bread in salt until it expanded, and then he ate it. Do we do that? No. Are we really displaying good manners towards food or not? We are not, because no one explained these things to us. You are excused if you didn't know, but now you are not excused. So I told Hajjah to bring a huge pot for us this evening—a pot of bread; let's see who will eat bread and who won't!

Sometimes you have very hot food or hot tea, but you have no right to blow on it as that is *harām*! It is not accepted. I found a way to quickly cool tea that is too hot to drink by putting ice cubes in it. Don't blow in the food or on warm or hot water.

Narrated by Ahmad ؓ, "Prophet advised you not to do that." And he is saying we must be patient until food comes to a temperature suitable to eat, so don't rush. The only time you are allowed to and must rush for food is when you are breaking fast in *Ramadan*. Then it is *sunnah* to rush. Don't be like non-Muslims, because they delay in their traditions, so break your fast immediately.

Don't drink while standing or laying down; Prophet prohibited that because you have to pull the drink down a little bit. Some people say it is narrated that Prophet drank while standing, but that applied only to ZamZam water; for respect you drink it standing because it is blessed water from heavens. May Allah forgive us and change our imitational fasting into real fasting by the blessings of Grandshaykh 'AbdAllah, Mawlana Shaykh Nazim ق and for the sake of Prophet ﷺ. *Amīn*.

Still we have to say *"alhamdulillah"* that Allah is sending His sincere servants here, coming for Allah ﷻ and His Prophet ﷺ. You are not coming for me, but for Mawlana Shaykh Nazim ق and Grandshaykh 'AbdAllah ق. There is no difference between us; we are all coming for the same purpose and all from same line, *Silsilat al-Rahmah*, the Chain of Mercy. Like family relationships, what we call *"silati 'r-rahm,"* *rahm* is a 'womb relationship' of brothers and sisters coming together. So all of us around the Internet and the world have one 'womb relationship' and all these benefits come from their sources.

I am nothing. We are sharing the love of Mawlana Shaykh ق. May Allah ﷻ keep that love and guide us and advise us, because such meetings are rare compared to pop culture in this world. What is rare makes you exist in His Existence!

May Allah ﷻ forgive us and may Allah ﷻ bless us.

Wa min Allahi 't-tawfiq, bi hurmati 'l-habīb, bi hurmati 'l-Fatihah.

And with Allah is success. For the sake of the Beloved, for his sake we recite the opening chapter of Holy Qur'an.

The Sin of Breaking the Fast of Ramadan Too Soon

*A'ūdhu billāhi min ash-Shaytani 'r-rajīm. Bismillāhi' r-Raḥmāni 'r-Raḥīm.
Nawaytu 'l-arbā'īn, nawaytu 'l-'itikāf, nawaytu'l-khalwah, nawaytu 'l-'uzlah,
nawaytu 'r-riyaḍa, nawaytu 's-sulūk, lillāhi Ta'alā fī hādhā 'l-masjid.
Ati'ūllāha wa ati'ū 'r-Rasūla wa ūli 'l-amri minkum.
Obey Allah, obey the Prophet, and obey those in authority among you. (4:59)*

Today is 30 *Ramadan* and for some it is 29 *Ramadan*. Anyone who did not fast twenty-nine days (the required minimum) and broke fast was wrong and deviant. They must fast and make up what they missed, and if they missed it intentionally, according to *Shari'ah*, for every day they missed they must fast for sixty consecutive days! Otherwise, if they broke the fast early without knowing it wasn't the end of *Ramadan* (i.e., if their leader told them to do so), they must fast and pay *kafārah*.

Those who knew better, but who broke the *Ramadan* fast before the end of the month are liable and will be held responsible in front of Allah ﷻ. For two missed days, they must fast 120 consecutive days. If some people cannot because of illness, they have to feed sixty poor people for each day they intentionally did not fast.

We do not agree with their decision to break fast early and are not responsible for what they did as they never asked us. If they had asked, we would have told them it was wrong and they would not have done it, but they did that without asking.

Those responsible have to fix this problem. Those who did not make that mistake, Allah ﷻ knows best about them.

People don't have minds! I told them they can fast from *Sha'bān*, no problem, and continue with *Ramadan*, because Sayyida A'yesha ؓ said, "I used to see the Prophet ﷺ fast the whole of *Sha'bān* or part of *Sha'bān*."

Then you continue, but you cannot break fast before your country breaks fast; you have to follow the rules of the religious authority of the country. Who are you to give the judgment and make 200 people go astray, equal to 400 days of consecutive fasts? We don't want to fall into this big trap of *Shaytan*! May Allah protect us and protect every Muslim.

May Allah ﷻ forgive us and may Allah ﷻ bless us.

Wa min Allahi 't-tawfīq, bi hurmati 'l-habīb, bi hurmati 'l-Fatihah.
And with Allah is success. For the sake of the Beloved, for his sake we recite the opening chapter of Holy Qur'an.

Islamic Calendar and Holy Days

The Islamic calendar is lunar-based, with twelve months of 29 or 30 days. A lunar year is shorter than a solar year, so Muslim holy days cycle back in the Gregorian (Western) calendar. This is how Ramadān is celebrated at different times of the year, as the annual Islamic calendar is ten days shorter than the Gregorian calendar.

Four Islamic months are sacred: Muharram, Rajab, Dhūl-Q'adah and Dhūl-Hijjah. Holy months include "God's Month" (Rajab), "Prophet's Month" (*Sha'bān*) and the "Month of the People" (Ramadān), in which pious acts are rewarded more generously.

Months of the Islamic Calendar

1. Muharram
2. Safar
3. Rabī' ul-Awwal (Rabī' I)
4. Rabī' uth-Thāni (Rabī' II)
5. Jumāda al-Awwal (Jumādi I)
6. Jumāda uth-Thāni (Jumādi II)
7. Rajab
8. *Sha'bān*
9. Ramadān
10. Shawwāl
11. Dhū'l-Q'adah
12. Dhū'l-Hijjah

al-Hijra

The 1st of Muharram marks the beginning of the Islamic New Year, chosen because it is the anniversary of Prophet Muhammad's ﷺ historic *hijrah* (migration) from Mecca to Madinah, where he established the first, preeminent Muslim community in which he introduced unprecedented social reforms, including civil law, human and women's rights, religious tolerance, taxation to serve the community, and military ethics.

'Ashura

1. On 10th Muharram, 'Ashura commemorates many sacred events, such as Noah's ark coming to rest, the birth of Abraham, and the building of the *Ka'bah* in Mecca. 'Ashura is a major holy day, marked with two days of fasting, on the $9^{th}/10^{th}$ or on $10^{th}/11^{th}$ based on a holy tradition (*hadīth*) of Sayyidina Muhammad ﷺ.

Mawlid

Mawlid al-Nabī, 12th Rabi' al-Awwal, commemorates Prophet Muhammad's birth in 570. Mawlid is celebrated globally throughout this month in huge communal gatherings in which a famous poem "Qasīdah al-Burdah" is recited, accompanied by drummers, illustrious poetry recitals, religious singing, eloquent sermons, gift giving, feasts, and feeding the poor. Most Muslim nations observe Mawlid as a national holiday.

Laylat al-Isra wal-Mi'raj

Literally, "the Night Journey and Ascension;" 27th of Rajab is when Sayyidina Muhammad ﷺ physically traveled from Mecca to Jerusalem, ascended in all the levels of Heaven from a rock in the Dome of the Rock, and returned to Mecca—while his bed was still warm. In the Night Journey, Islam's five daily prayers were ordained by God. Sayyidina Muhammad ﷺ also prayed with Abraham, Moses, and Jesus in Jerusalem's al-Aqsa Mosque, signifying that Muslims, Christians, and Jews follow one god. This holy event designated Jerusalem as the third holiest site in Islam, after Mecca and Madinah.

Laylat al-Bara'ah

The "Night of Freedom from Fire" occurs on 15th *Sha'bān*. On this night God's Mercy is great; hence, the night is spent reciting Holy Qur'an and special prayers, as well as visiting the deceased.

Ramadan

Many regard Ramadān, the 9th month of the Islamic calendar, the holiest month of the year. Muslims observe a strict fast and participate in pious activities such as charitable giving and peace making. It is a time of intense spiritual renewal for those who observe it. Fasting is meant to instill social awareness of the needy, and to promote gratitude for God's endless favors. The fast is typically broken in a communal setting, and hence Ramadān is a highly social month. At night, a special Ramadān prayer known as "Tarawīh" is offered in congregation, in which one-thirtieth of the Holy Qur'an is recited by the *imam* (prayer leader); thus the entire holy book of 6,000 verses is recited in this month.

Eid al-Fitr

"Festival of Fast-Breaking" marks the end of Ramadān and is celebrated the first three days of Shawwāl. It is a time for charity and celebration with family and friends for completing a month of blessings and joy. In the Last Days of Ramadān, each Muslim family gives "*Zakat al-Fitr*"(charity of fast-breaking) which consists of cash and/or food, to help the poor. On the first early morning of Eid, Muslims observe a special congregational prayer, such as Christmas/Easter Mass or the High Holy Days. After Eid prayer is a time to visit family and friends, and give gifts and money (especially to children). Many specialty foods and sweets are prepared solely for Eid days. In most Muslim countries, the entire three days of Eid is a national holiday.

Yawm al-Arafat

"Day of 'Arafat," the 9th Dhul-Hijjah, occurs just before the celebration of Eid al-Adha. Pilgrims on *Hajj* assemble for the "standing" on the plain of 'Arafat, located outside Mecca, where they contemplate the Day of Standing (Resurrection Day). Muslims elsewhere in the world fast this day, and gather at a local mosque for prayers. Thus, those who cannot perform *Hajj* that year still honor the sacrifice of Abraham.

Eid al-Adha

The "Feast of Sacrifice," celebrated from the 10th-13th Dhul-Hijjah, marks Prophet Abraham's willingness to sacrifice his son Ismā'īl on God's order. To honor this event, Muslims perform *Hajj*, the pilgrimage to Mecca that is incumbent on every mature Muslim once in their life if they have the means. Celebrations begin with an animal sacrifice to commemorate Sayyidina Abraham's sacrifice. In Islam, he is known as *Khalilullāh*, "God's friend." Many consider him the first Muslim and a premiere role model, for his obedience to God and willingness to sacrifice his only child without even questioning the command.

Glossary

'abd (pl. *'ibād*): slave; servant.
'AbdAllah: Lit., "servant of God."
Abu Bakr as-Siddīq: the closest Companion of Prophet Muhammad; the Prophet's father-in-law who shared the *Hijra* with him. After the Prophet's death, he was elected the first caliph (successor); known as one of the most saintly Companions.
Abu Yazīd/Bayazīd Bistāmī: A great ninth century *wali* and a master of the Naqshbandi Golden Chain.
adab: good manners, proper etiquette.
adhān: call to prayer.
Ahlu 'l-Bayt: "People of the House;" Prophet Muhammad's family and descendants.
Ākhirah: the Hereafter; afterlife.
al-: Arabic definite article, "the".
'alāmīn: world; universes.
Alhamdulillah: praise God.
'Ali ibn Abi Talib: first cousin of Prophet Muhammad, married to his daughter Fatimah; the fourth caliph.
alif: first letter of Arabic alphabet.
'Alim, al-: the Knower, a divine attribute
Allah: proper name for God in Arabic.
Allahu Akbar: God is Greater.
'āmal: good deed (pl. *'amāl*).
amīr (pl., *umarā*): chief, leader, head of a nation or people.
anā: first person singular pronoun
anbiya: prophets (sing. *nabi*).
'aql: intellect, reason; from the root *'aqila* lit., "to fetter."
'Arafah, 'Arafat: a plain near Mecca where pilgrims gather for the principal rite of *Hajj*.

'arif: knower, Gnostic; one who has reached spiritual knowledge of his Lord.
'Ārifūn' bil-Lāh: knowers of God.
Ar-Rahīm: The Mercy-Giving, Merciful, Munificent, one of Allah's ninety-nine Holy Names.
Ar-Rahmān: The Most Merciful, Compassionate, Beneficent; the most repeated of Allah's Holy Names.
'arsh, al-: the Divine Throne.
asl: root, origin, basis.
astaghfirullah: lit. "I seek Allah's forgiveness."
Awliyaullah: saints of Allah (sing. *wali*).
āyah (pl. *ayat*): a verse of the Holy Qur'an.
Āyat al-Kursi: "Verse of the Throne," a well-known supplication from the Qur'an (2:255).
'Azra'īl: the Archangel of Death.
Badī' al-: The Innovator; a divine name.
Banī Adam: Children of Adam; humanity.
Bayt al-Maqdis: the Sacred Mosque in Jerusalem, built at the site where Solomon's Temple was later erected.
Bayt al-Mā'mūr: much-frequented house; this refers to the *Ka'bah* of the heavens, which is the prototype of the *Ka'bah* on earth, circumambulated by the angels.
baya': pledge; in the context of this book, the pledge of initiation of a disciple (*murīd*) to a Shaykh.
Bismillāhi'r-Rahmāni'r-Rahīm: "In the name of the All-Merciful, the All-Compassionate"; introductory verse

to all chapters of the Qur'an, except the ninth.

Dajjāl: the False Messiah (Anti-Christ) will appear at the end-time of this world, to deceive mankind with false divinity.

dalālah: evidence.

dhāt: self / selfhood.

dhawq (pl. *adhwāq*): tasting; technical term referring to the experiential aspect of gnosis.

dhikr: remembrance, mention of God in His Holy Names or phrases of glorification.

ḍīya: light.

Diwān al-Awliya: the nightly gathering of saints with Prophet Muhammad in the spiritual realm.

du'ā: supplication.

dunya: world; worldly life.

'Eid: festival; the two major celebrations of Islam are 'Eid al-Fitr, after Ramadān; and 'Eid al-Adha, the Festival of Sacrifice during the time of *Hajj*, which commemorates the sacrifice of Prophet Abraham.

fard: obligatory worship.

Fatihah: *Suratu 'l-Fatihah*; the opening chapter of the Qur'an.

Ghafūr, al-: The Forgiver; one of the Holy Names of God.

ghawth: lit. "Helper"; the highest rank of all saints.

ghaybu' l-mutlaq, al-: the Absolute Unknown; known only to God.

ghusl: full shower/bath obligated by a state of ritual impurity, performed before worship.

Grandshaykh: generally, a *wali* of great stature. In this text, refers to Mawlana 'AbdAllah ad-Daghestāni (d. 1973), Mawlana Shaykh Nazim's master.

hā': the Arabic letter ه

hadīth Nabawī (pl., *ahadīth*): prophetic *hadīth* whose meaning and linguistic expression are those of Prophet Muhammad.

Hadīth Qudsī: divine saying whose meaning directly reflects the meaning God intended but whose linguistic expression is not divine speech as in the Qur'an.

hadr: present

Hajj: the sacred pilgrimage of Islam obligatory on every mature Muslim once in their life.

halal: permitted, lawful according to Islamic *Sharī'ah*.

haqīqah, al-: reality of existence; ultimate truth.

haqq: truth

Haqq, al-: the Divine Reality, one of the 99 Divine Names.

harām: forbidden, unlawful.

hasanāt: good deeds.

hāshā: God forbid.

harf: (pl. *hurūf*) letter; Arabic root "edge."

Hawā: Eve.

haywān: animal.

Hijra: emigration.

hikmah: wisdom.

hujjah: proof.

hūwa: the pronoun "he," made up of the Arabic letters *hā'* and *wāw*.

'ibādu 'l-Lāh: servants of God.

'ifrīt: a type of Jinn, huge and powerful.

ihsān: doing good, "It is to worship God as though you see Him; for if you are not seeing Him, He sees you."

ikhlās, al-: sincere devotion.

ilāh: (pl. *āliha*): idols or gods.

ilāhīyya: divinity.

ilhām: divine inspiration sent to *awliyaullah*.

ʿilm: knowledge, science.
ʿIlmu 'l-Awrāq: Knowledge of Papers.
ʿIlmu 'l-Adhwāq: Knowledge of Taste.
ʿIlmu 'l-Hurūf: Knowledge of the Science of Letters.
ʿIlmu 'l-Kalām: scholastic Theology.
ʿIlmun Ladunnī: divinely inspired Knowledge.
imān: faith, belief.
imam: leader of congregational prayer; an advanced scholar followed by a large community.
insān: humanity; pupil of the eye.
Insānu 'l-Kāmil, al-: the Perfect Man, i.e., Prophet Muhammad.
irādatullāh: the Will of God.
irshād: spiritual guidance.
ism: name.
isma-Llāh: name of God.
isrāʿ: night journey; used here in reference to the night journey of Prophet Muhammad.
Isrāʿfīl: Archangel Rafael, in charge of blowing the Final Trumpet.
jalāl: majesty.
jamāl: beauty.
jamaʿa: group, congregation.
Jannah: Paradise.
jihād: to struggle in God's Path.
Jibrīl: Gabriel, Archangel of revelation.
Jinn: a species of living beings created from fire, invisible to most humans. Jinn can be Muslims or non-Muslims.
Jumuʿah: Friday congregational prayer, held in a large mosque.
Kaʿbah: the first House of God, located in Mecca, Saudi Arabia to which pilgrimage is made and to which Muslims face in prayer.
kāfir: unbeliever.
Kalāmullāh al-Qadīm: lit., Allah's Ancient Words, viz. the Holy Qur'an.

kalīmat at-tawhīd: Lā ilāha illa-Llāh: "There is no god but Al-Lah (the God)."
karāmat: miracles.
khalīfah: deputy.
Khāliq, al-: the Creator, one of 99 Divine Names.
khalq: creation.
khāniqa: designated smaller place for worship other than a mosque; zāwiya.
khuluq: conduct, manners.
Kirāmun Kātabīn: honored Scribe angels.
lā: no; not; not existent; the particle of negation.
Lā ilāha illa-Llāh Muhammadun Rasūlullah: There is no deity except Allah, Muhammad is the Messenger of Allah.
lām: Arabic letter ل
al-Lawh al-Mahfūz: the Preserved Tablets.
Laylat al-Isrāʿ waʾl-Miʿrāj: the Night Journey and Ascension of Prophet Muhammad to Jerusalem and to the Seven Heavens.
Madīnātu 'l-Munawwara: the Illuminated city; city of Prophet Muhammad; Madinah.
mahr: dowry, given by the groom to the bride.
malakūt: divine kingdom.
Malik, al-: the Sovereign, a divine name.
Mālik: Archangel of Hell.
maqām: spiritual station; tomb of a prophet, messenger or saint.
maʿrifah: gnosis.
Masha'Allah: as Allah Wills.
Mawlana: lit. "Our master" or "our patron," referring to an esteemed person.
mazhar: place of disclosure.
mihrāb: prayer niche.

Mikā'īl: Michael, Archangel of rain.
mīzān: the scale that weighs our deeds on Judgment Day.
mīm: Arabic letter م.
minbar: pulpit.
Miracles: of saints, known as *karamāt*; of prophets, known as *mu'jizāt* (lit., "That which renders powerless or helpless").
mi'rāj: the ascension of Prophet Muhammad from Jerusalem to the Seven Heavens.
Muhammadun Rasūlullah: Muhammad is the Messenger of God.
mulk, al-: the World of dominion.
Mu'min, al-: Guardian of Faith, one of the 99 Names of God.
mu'min: a believer.
munājāt: invocation to God in a very intimate form.
Munkir: one of the angels of the grave.
murīd: disciple, student, follower.
murshid: spiritual guide; *pir*.
mushāhada: direct witnessing.
mushrik (pl. *mushrikūn*): idolater; polytheist.
muwwāhid (pl. *muwāhhidūn*): those who affirm God's Oneness.
nabī: a prophet of God.
nafs: lower self, ego.
Nakīr: the other angel of the grave (with Munkir).
nūr: light.
Nūh: the prophet Noah.
Nūr, an-: "The Source of Light"; a divine name.
Qādir, al-: "The Powerful"; a divine name.
qalam, al-: the Pen.
qiblah: direction, specifically, the direction faced by Muslims during prayer and other worship, towards the Sacred House in Mecca.

Quddūs, al-: "The Holy One"; a divine name.
qurb: nearness
qutb (pl. *aqtāb*): axis or pole. Among the poles are:
 Qutb al-Bilād: Pole of the Lands.
 Qutb al-Irshād: Pole of Guidance.
 Qutb al-Aqtāb: Pole of Poles.
 Qutb al-Azham: Highest Pole.
 Qutb al-Mutasarrif: Pole of Affairs.
al-Qutbīyyatu 'l-Kubrā: the highest Station of Poleship.
Rabb, ar-: the Lord.
Rahīm, ar-: "The Most Compassionate"; a divine name.
Rahmān, ar-: "The All-Merciful"; a divine name.
rahmā: mercy.
raka'at: one full set of prescribed motions in prayer. Each prayer consists of a one or more *raka'ats*.
Ramadān: the ninth month of the Islamic calendar; month of fasting.
Rasūl: a messenger of God.
Rasūlullah: the Messenger of God, Muhammad ﷺ.
Ra'ūf, ar-: "The Most Kind"; a divine name.
Razzāq, ar-: "The Provider"; a divine name.
rawhānīyyah: spirituality; spiritual essence of something.
Ridwān: Archangel of Paradise.
rizq: provision; sustenance.
rūh: spirit. *Ar-Rūh* is the name of a great angel.
rukū': bowing posture of the prayer.
sadaqah: voluntary charity.
Sahābah (sing., *sahābī*): Companions of the Prophet; the first Muslims.
sahīh: authentic; term certifying validity of a *hadīth* of the Prophet.
sāim: fasting person (pl. *sāimūn*)
sajda (pl. *sujūd*): prostration.

salāt: ritual prayer, one of the five obligatory pillars of Islam. Also, to invoke blessing on the Prophet.
Salāt an-Najāt: prayer of salvation, offered in the late hours of night.
salawāt (sing. *salāt*): invoking blessings and peace upon the Prophet.
salam: peace.
Salam, as-: "The Peaceful"; a divine name. *As-salamu 'alaykum*: "Peace be upon you," the Islamic greeting.
Samad, as-: Self-Sufficient, upon whom creatures depend.
sawm, siyam: fasting.
sayyi'āt: bad deeds; sins.
sayyid: leader; also, a descendant of Prophet Muhammad.
Sayyidina: our master (fem. *sayyidunā*; *sayyidatunā*: our mistress).
shahādah: lit. testimony; the testimony of Islamic faith: *lā ilāha illa 'l-Lāh wa Muhammadun Rasūlullah*, "There is no god but Allah, the One God, and Muhammad is the Messenger of God."
Shah Naqshband: Muhammad Bahauddin Shah Naqshband, a great eighth century wali, and the founder of the Naqshbandi Tarīqah.
Shaykh: lit. "old Man," a religious guide, teacher; master of spiritual discipline.
shifā': cure.
shirk: polytheism, idolatry, ascribing partners to God
Siffāt: attributes; term referring to Divine Attributes.
Silsilat adh-Dhahabīyya: "Golden Chain" of spiritual authority in Islam
sohbet (Arabic, *suhbah*): association: the assembly or discourse of a Shaykh.
SubhanAllah: glory be to God.

sultān/sultāna: ruler, monarch.
Sultan al-Awliya: lit., "King of the *awliya*; the highest-ranking saint.
Sūnnah: Practices of Prophet Muhammad in actions and words; what he did, said, recommended, or approved of in his Companions.
sūrah: a chapter of the Qur'an; picture, image.
Suratu 'l-Ikhlās: Chapter 114 of Holy Qur'an; the Chapter of Sincerity.
tabīb: doctor.
tābi'īn: the Successors, one generation after the Prophet's Companions.
tafsīr: to explain, expound, explicate, or interpret; technical term for commentary or exegesis of the Holy Qur'an.
tajallī (pl. *tajallīyat*): theophany, God's self-disclosures, Divine Self-manifestation.
takbīr: lit. "Allahu Akbar," God is Great.
tarawīh: the special nightly prayers of Ramadān.
tarīqat/tarīqah: lit., way, road or path. An Islamic order or path of discipline and devotion under a guide or Shaykh; Sufism.
tasbih: recitation glorifying or praising God.
tawāda': humbleness.
tawāf: the rite of circumambulating the Ka'bah while glorifying God during *Hajj* and *'Umra*.
tawhīd: unity; universal or primordial Islam, submission to God, as the sole Master of destiny and ultimate Reality.
Tawrāt: Torah
tayammum: Alternate ritual ablution performed in the absence of water.
'ubūdīyyah: state of worshipfulness. Servanthood

'ulamā (sing. *'ālim*): scholars.
'Ulūm al-Awwalīna wa 'l-Ākhirīn: Knowledge of the "Firsts" and the "Lasts," refers to the knowledge God poured into the heart of Prophet Muhammad during his ascension to the Divine Presence.
'Ulūm al-Islāmī: Islamic religious sciences.
Ummāh: faith community, nation.
'Umar ibn al-Khattāb: an eminent Companion of Prophet Muhammad and second caliph of Islam.
'Umra: the minor pilgrimage to Mecca, performed at any time of the year.
'Uthmān ibn 'Affān: eminent Companion of the Prophet; his son-in-law and third caliph of Islam, renowned for compiling the Qur'an.
walad: a child.
waladī: my child.
walāyah: proximity or closeness; sainthood.
wali (pl. *awliya*): saint, or "he who assists"; guardian; protector.

wasīlah: a means; holy station of Prophet Muhammad as God's intermediary to grant supplications.
wāw: Arabic letter
wujūd, al-: existence; "to find," "the act of finding," and "being found."
Y'aqūb: Jacob; the prophet.
yamīn: the right hand; previously meant "oath."
Yawm al-'Ahdi wa'l-Mīthāq: Day of Oath and Covenant, a heavenly event before this Life when all souls of humanity were presented to God and He took from each the promise to accept His Sovereignty as Lord.
Yawm al-Qiyamah: Day of Judgment.
Yūsuf: Joseph; the prophet.
zāwiya: designated smaller place for worship other than a mosque; also *khāniqa*.
zīyara: visitation to the grave of a prophet, a prophet's companion or a saint.

Other Publications / www.isn1.net

Mawlana Shaykh Nazim Adil al-Haqqani

Heavenly Showers (2012)
The Sufilive Series (2010-2011)
Breaths from Beyond the Curtain (2010)
In the Eye of the Needle
The Healing Power of Sufi Meditation
The Path to Spiritual Excellence
In the Mystic Footsteps of Saints (2 volumes)
Liberating the Soul (6 volumes)

Shaykh Hisham Kabbani

The Prohibition of Domestic Violence in Islam (2011)
The Sufilive Series (2010-2011)
Cyprus Summer Series (2 volumes)
The Nine-fold Ascent
Who Are the Guides?
Illuminations
Banquet for the Soul
Symphony of Remembrance
The Healing Power of Sufi Meditation
In the Shadow of Saints
Keys to the Divine Kingdom
The Sufi Science of Self-Realization
Universe Rising: the Approach of Armageddon?
Pearls and Coral (2 volumes)
Classical Islam and the Naqshbandi Sufi Tradition
The Naqshbandi Sufi Way
Encyclopedia of Islamic Doctrine (7 volumes)
Angels Unveiled
Encyclopedia of Muhammad's Women Companions and the Traditions They Related

Hajjah Amina Adil

Muhammad ﷺ: the Messenger of Islam
The Light of Muhammad ﷺ
Lore of Light / Links of Light
My Little Lore of Light (3 volumes)

Hajjah Naziha Adil Kabbani

Secrets of Heavenly Food (2009)
Heavenly Foods (2010)

www.ingramcontent.com/pod-product-compliance
Lightning Source LLC
Chambersburg PA
CBHW020418080526
44584CB00014B/1384